A Century of Jewelry
Classy, Flashy, and Trashy!

Deborah Crosby

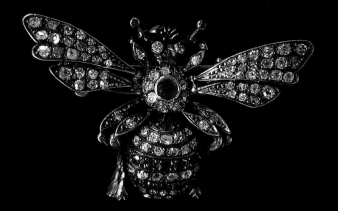

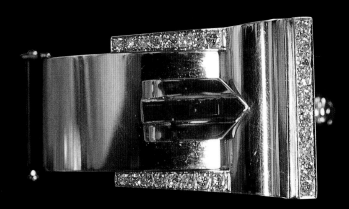

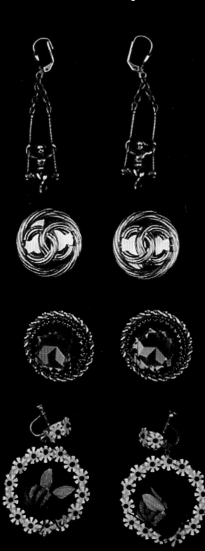

Schiffer Publishing Ltd

4880 Lower Valley Road, Atglen, PA 19310 USA

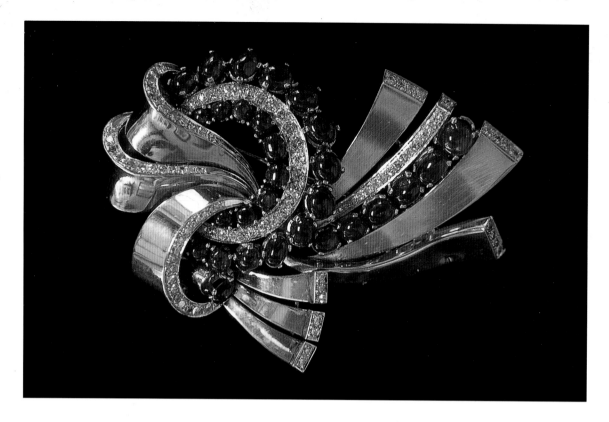

Library of Congress Cataloging-in-Publication Data

Crosby, Deborah.
  A century of jewelry : classy, flashy, and trashy! / Deborah
Crosby.
    p. cm.
  Includes bibliographical references and index.
  ISBN 0-7643-2323-7 (hardcover)
1. Jewelry—Collectors and collecting. I. Title.
  NK7304.C76 2005
  739.27'075—dc22
                                        2005018820

Photography by Deborah Crosby

Designed by John P. Cheek
Cover design by Bruce Waters
Cover photo composed by Deborah Crosby
Type set in UniversityRoman Bd BT/Humanist 521 BT

ISBN: 0-7643-2323-7
Printed in China
1 2 3 4

Published by Schiffer Publishing Ltd.
4880 Lower Valley Road
Atglen, PA 19310
Phone: (610) 593-1777; Fax: (610) 593-2002
E-mail: Info@schifferbooks.com

For the largest selection of fine reference books on this
and related subjects, please visit our web site at
www.schifferbooks.com
We are always looking for people to write books on
new and related subjects. If you have an idea for a book
please contact us at the above address.

This book may be purchased from the publisher.
Include $3.95 for shipping.
Please try your bookstore first.
You may write for a free catalog.

In Europe, Schiffer books are distributed by
Bushwood Books
6 Marksbury Ave.
Kew Gardens
Surrey TW9 4JF England
Phone: 44 (0) 20 8392-8585;
Fax: 44 (0) 20 8392-9876
E-mail: info@bushwoodbooks.co.uk
Free postage in the U.K., Europe; air mail at cost.

Dedication

To Nin and Gramp—thanks for being nice to that jeweler. To my family and friends for loving me even though I spend more time doing research than I do socializing. To Em— the gems you planted have taken root and are still growing.

Acknowledgments

Maris Durland, Rachel Durland, Ed Heller, Thomas Y. Hobart, Jr., Em Kuna. Vicki Bonanno, Marilyn Brookwood, Charles Cohn, Marcia Coltin, Gail Crockett, Gail Enos, Mary Ferrante, Adele Golden of Garden Gate Antiques, Ron Hoffman, the Kuna family, Kenneth Jay Lane, Jack and Kathleen Leone, Rachel Marks, Kathy Milliken, Vita Materasso, John McKenzie, Scott Mikolay and the ladies at Desires, Chris Petrillo, Ellen Pincus, Anna Reis, Christie Romero, Ruth Taylor, Beverly Houghton, Giselle De Rienzo Antiques, Gerald Schultz of the Antique Gallery, Tom and Mary Valentino of Others' Oldies, Bonnie Yankauer, and to those who wish to remain anonymous. Some of you shared your jewelry and some of you shared your love, and all of you made this book possible. My sincere thanks.

Contents

Introduction

Collecting in and of itself is a fascinating study. Something catches your eye, perhaps a necklace with big blue stones and a delicate silver chain. Maybe your birthday is in September and the sapphire is your birthstone, maybe the necklace is in a box of objects marked fifty cents each. Before you know it, you're hooked. You pay the fifty cents, without even bargaining. You realize that the chain is broken and fixing it will cost more than the initial investment but still decide it's worth it. You withstand the criticism of a boyfriend (now long-gone) who questions your wisdom in spending fifty cents for a broken necklace. You privately wonder about its age and who owned it (clearly not sharing any of these romantic notions with the insensitive dummy you've mistakenly brought to an antiques show). Looking at the necklace, you fantasize about a different lifestyle and imagine the necklace to consist of real sapphires and real pearls, even though you are fully aware that the stones are glass and that it would be unlikely to see yellowed glue holding genuine pearls. It seems to be made of silver, though, and you have just spent the past four weeks saving up to buy a handcrafted silver ring, which, at twenty dollars, took not only budgeting the allowance but lots of hours of babysitting at fifty cents an hour.

You decide it's a fair trade, an hour with a bunch of kids for an antique necklace and a world of imagination. It's actually a bargain.

Bringing the piece to a jewelers for repair requires listening to many who say it's not worth the time. Finding someone who will take the time to fabricate a link or two to match the originals is complicated, especially considering that you don't have your driver's license yet and that you have to walk everywhere.

Finding a cooperative jeweler in your hometown, though, is exciting. Even if you're vaguely aware that he's helping you because your grandparents not only buy gifts from him, but that he also makes their eyeglasses and thinks they are very nice people, you still feel honored that at least a few adults don't think you're foolish. You wait the weeks it takes for the repair, you save up to pay for it, and you are thrilled at the results. The necklace is intact and now can be worn.

Having it repaired means you have to find a way to wear it, a dress to wear it with, an event appropriate for an old silver necklace that's not exactly inconspicuous. A few years later, at college, such an event does arise and you're happy to be able to wear this wonderful necklace with a gown, finally. Attending a ball in the historic Hall of Springs in Saratoga Springs, you feel like a very wise person for having purchased the necklace, and you feel almost historically correct wearing a vintage piece of jewelry in the old ballroom, albeit a room filled with young women (dancing with their fathers on Father-Daughter weekend) wearing nothing vaguely like what you have around your neck.

Seeing the necklace decades later will remind you that you were young and idealistic and romantic and, despite the intervening decades, you realize that besides not being exactly young anymore, you are still idealistic and romantic. Your own daughters beg you to wear it as they ask you to pose for a series of nostalgic photographs they've envisioned. They, too, have been captivated by the glittering stones and the graceful silver tracery, and are intrigued by a piece of jewelry that their mother bought for fifty cents when she was just about their age.

Still later, you're asked to write a book about jewelry, and you realize that it's an enormously large topic. Despite your enthusiasm, you are almost overwhelmed with the amount of information that's available, the vast variety of jewelry that's been created and the fact that, no matter how much you learn, by the time the book is finished you will only have scratched the surface. Learning about jewelry will be a lifetime pursuit. So you decide to try to recapture what it felt like to be a novice, a beginner, a child with fifty cents and an awful lot of optimism.

Old jewelry still has its hold, the attraction is still there and the reasons for the attraction are still valid. Old jewelry is beguiling. And fifty cents won't buy me much today, but if I try to see with unjaded eyes, I can still find treasures.

Bohemian glass and silver festoon necklace, circa 1910.

One Hundred Years of Jewelry:
Classy, Flashy, and Trashy!

Writing this book took much longer than I anticipated. There is far more to learn than I acknowledged initially, and of course I didn't expect to spend the better part of a year recovering from an illness that was exacerbated by, of all things, materials used to make jewelry. Yet, despite these complications, writing this book has been a great adventure. Studying jewelry has enlightened me, intrigued me, and captivated me. Jewelry is everywhere, and there is so much to learn that one could devote a lifetime to the study and still not learn everything there is to know. I have limited this book to encompass a one hundred year period in order to reduce the scope and to make it possible to include several examples of the many styles that went in and out of favor during that period of time. Much of the actual jewelry, as well as evidence of the history of jewelry in America from the 1860s to the 1960s, is accessible and tangible, especially if the focus is on jewelry made of materials that were newly created substitutes for the "real thing." Among the reasons that this period is so interesting are the scale of exploration, the rate of success that was attained by inventors and manufacturers, and the rapidity of change that occurred as a result. Finding new materials to use in jewelry manufacturing so that it could be more affordable and more widely available is a form of nineteenth and twentieth century alchemy, in a sense. The quest to create suitable substitutes for precious metals and gems coalesced during this period. Although there are certainly examples of faux diamonds and pearls prior to this time, the sheer numbers of discoveries, the ability to mechanize and realize the potential of those discoveries, and the acceptance of these alternatives accelerated the process as never before. The end products are sometimes classy, sometimes flashy, and even sometimes trashy, but they are always interesting!

Visual Timeline

*I*n order to enable the reader to gain a greater understanding of the jewelry that was created during this hundred year period, this book begins with a visual timeline. I've included several images for each decade to illustrate how the world changed over the years from 1860 to 1910. In addition to examples of jewelry, the reader will also find an original drawing or painting that was created during each decade or so, as well as photographs that allow us a glimpse of how people lived during that era. For example, between 1890 and 1910, many women wore prim, long dresses with mutton-chop sleeves. But the Art Nouveau movement also depicted women as sensuous (and in the example on page 18, quite naked!) beings. Women during this time period took up bicycle riding, playing golf, and smoking cigarettes. Wealthier women used their leisure time to draw. It is easier, I think, to envision a woman wearing an Art Nouveau brooch if you can envision what she was like, how she lived, what her world was like. When these images are compared to those drawn or photographed a mere ten years later, the change is often quite striking. While eras generally don't begin exactly on one particular date, and while there is always some continuity from one era to the next, it is helpful to note the differences in styles between one decade and the next.

The values for the jewelry in the timeline are listed in the caption with each individual piece later in this book. Values are approximate, and it is possible that you will find the same pin or bracelet or earrings (etcetera) for more or less than the value range listed here. These prices are based on the listed prices for the same or comparable items at antiques and collectibles shops and shows, and research on the internet. Dealers have been consulted, as have collectors. As we all know, pricing is an art as much as it is an imperfect science.

1850s-1880s: *left to right, top to bottom:* Black ebonite chain (16") and teardrop-shaped pendant (2") with gadrooned edges and Dionysian portrait, unmarked. Prong-set faceted garnets and silver brooch (2" x 1/2"), with simple C hasp and tube hinge, unmarked. Silver ladies watch chain, heart-shaped slider with turquoise stone (approximately 48"). Gun metal chain (50") with locket, unmarked. Intricately carved lava cameo earrings (limestone), gold bezels and kidney wires, male and female busts face each other (approximately 1" x 3/4" not including wire), unmarked. Silver medallion cufflinks, marked "Acme" patented August 24, 1880. Gold ladies watch chain, with slide engraved "I. E. H." and cast hand holding hinged bail (58"), unmarked. Floral ornament made of different colors of human hair and green glass beads. Vulcanite or ebonite (black hard rubber) and gold bracelet, unmarked. Sterling silver watch chain, hallmarked on each link (16"). Whitby jet cameo (1 1/2" x 1"). Silver telescoping dip pen and mechanical pencil with case, marked "Sterling."

Pen and ink drawing by an anonymous artist. Men turn their heads to gaze at a stylish young woman as she sweeps past a shop window. She is wearing a crinoline, a structured undergarment which creates the bell-like appearance of her skirt (circa 1850).

Stereograph of buffalo. By the 1860s buffalo were already disappearing. Nonetheless, this image helps to put American jewelry and fashion in context.

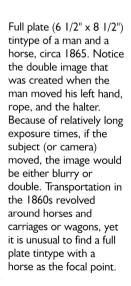

Full plate (6 1/2" x 8 1/2") tintype of a man and a horse, circa 1865. Notice the double image that was created when the man moved his left hand, rope, and the halter. Because of relatively long exposure times, if the subject (or camera) moved, the image would be either blurry or double. Transportation in the 1860s revolved around horses and carriages or wagons, yet it is unusual to find a full plate tintype with a horse as the focal point.

Far left:
Queen Victoria reigned from 1837-1903.

Left:
Photograph of a young woman wearing a jet necklace and earrings, a gold or silver brooch. Circa 1870.

Carte de visite of a young woman with long, loose hair, wearing earrings and an elaborate necklace with a center pendant and two tassels. Photo marked Noble's Gallery, Kissel, No. 328 Delaware Street, Leavenworth, Kansas. Circa 1870.

Hand-colored fashion plate, "Godey's Fashions for November 1868."

Scenes from the life of a typical Victorian woman: Monday was laundry day, Tuesday was the day for ironing, Wednesday was the day for sewing, Thursday one "made calls," Friday the house was scrubbed, and Saturday was set aside for baking. Sunday was the day of rest. Circa 1890, from a Victorian scrapbook. On Monday, a boy and girl play—the boy floats a toy boat in the washtub as the girl takes care of her doll. On Tuesday, Wednesday, and Saturday, children help with the chores.

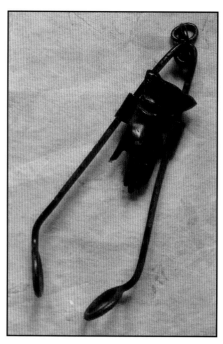

This clip was designed to hold a woman's skirt while she danced.

This photograph shows a ship passing through the newly opened Suez Canal.

The Centennial Exposition in Philadelphia (1876).

Trade card influenced by the opera *Aida*.

1870s-1890s: *left to right, top to bottom:* Gold pencil with turquoise slide, with British registration marks (worn and illegible), 2 1/2" x 1/2" open. Gold and silver magic pencil with bust of Julius Caesar, marked "Fairchild" (American), 2 1/2" x 1/2" open. Hand-carved, translucent cameo, 800 silver (marked) and gold twisted wire bezel, with both pin and bail (can be worn as a pendant or brooch), 1" x 3/4". Three-color gold scarf pin in the Japanese style. The gold band has a "bloom" finish, and the details of the appliqué green gold bird's wings and feathers and rose gold grasses are hand-engraved (1" x 1/4" x 3/4"). Unmarked, but of the quality and the style of jewelry made by Tiffany in the 1870s (see page 26, jewelry designed by Edward Moore, *Tiffany Fauna*). Hand-painted enamel pharaoh, set in low-carat gold, cufflink, 1". Mixed metal magic pencil watch fob/charm in the form of a woman wearing a kimono, holding a fan (probably modeled after Okame). Marked "Edward Todd & Co.," 2 1/4" open. Rolled gold watch chain, 17". Sterling silver and paste bull dog, with French punch mark (fleur-de-lis with crown), 1" x 3/4", repoussé top with hand-set stones and pierced, appliquéd on top of a back with pierced area behind the head to allow ruby eyes to catch more light, very heavy for its size. Three tiered opal pendant with hand-engraved gold bezels and pierced settings. Mixed metals chatelaine holder, in the Japanese style. Marked "Sterling F. B." (3 1/2" x 1"). Silver and gold magic pencil watch fob/charm in the form of an urn, marked "Edward Todd & Co. N. Y." (1 1/2" x 3/4"). Vest pocket pencil, silver with French punch mark; owl sitting in a pine tree and crescent moon on one side, two love birds sitting in a holly tree and rising sun on the reverse (3 1/2" x 1/4"). Niello silver and gold watch chain, 27", unmarked. Graduated coral cabochons set onto a brass brooch in the shape of a horse shoe (1 1/4" x 1 1/2"). Gilded belt buckle incorporating coin and die-stamped pieces embellished with dolphins; amethysts set in crenellated bezels (2" x 4 1/4").

13

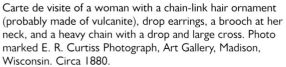

Carte de visite of a woman with a chain-link hair ornament (probably made of vulcanite), drop earrings, a brooch at her neck, and a heavy chain with a drop and large cross. Photo marked E. R. Curtiss Photograph, Art Gallery, Madison, Wisconsin. Circa 1880.

Top right:
Stereographic view of Chestnut Street in Philadelphia, circa 1890. While street cars and power lines are clearly in use at the time this photograph was taken, it is also obvious that the streets are also shared with horse-drawn carriages. Many jewelers were, and still are, located on Chestnut Street.

Pocket watch and friendship token bracelet, circa 1870. Bracelet has Canadian coins burnished and engraved with names and initials on the reverse. $250-$300.

1890s-1910: Silver brooches, both hand-engraved and unmarked (top, 1 1/4" x 1", bottom 1"). Gilded buckle with green stones set in open bezels on a repoussé pattern with roses and stylized waves, with flat sheet soldered on the back, marked "Sterling" (4" x 2"). Gold pin with seed pearls, in the form of a bunch of grapes with rose gold branch and vine, and yellow gold, hand-engraved leaves (1" x 3/4"). Art Nouveau scarf pin in the shape of a snake with its tail looped around its head, ruby eyes, gold with punch mark (1" x 3/4"). Art Nouveau pin, girl with flowing hair, hat, and middy tie, marked "Sterling" (1 1/4" x 1"). Art Nouveau pin, mixed metals, young woman in water with lily pads (2 1/4" x 1 3/4"), unmarked. Mixed metal choker with appliquéd frogs, turtles, crescent moons, shells, dogs, bats, owls, cherries on simulated hand-hammered mounts (14" x 1"), unmarked. Silver book chain (16" x 1/2") with drop (2" x 1/2") and locket die-stamped and hand engraved (1 1/2" x 2"), hallmarked W. A., Birmingham (anchor), 1890 (Gothic "q").

Hardcover catalog, William J. Fraser, Lincoln, Pennsylvania, 1892. At 722 pages, this catalog illustrates a vast array of silver, silver plate, jewelry, and watches offered for sale by the "busiest house in America." All the illustrations are done from drawings, photographs are not yet in use in catalogs. $125-$150.

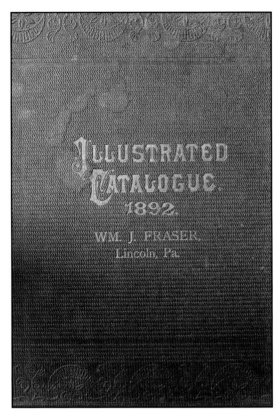

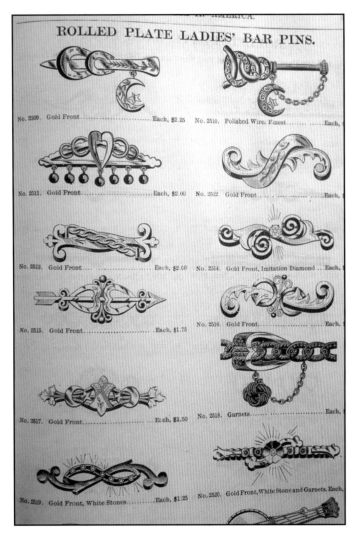

Page from Fraser catalog illustrating "gold emblem lapel buttons." Pages such as these help identify the fraternal organizations represented by different symbols.

Illustration of rolled plate ladies bar pins, page 659.

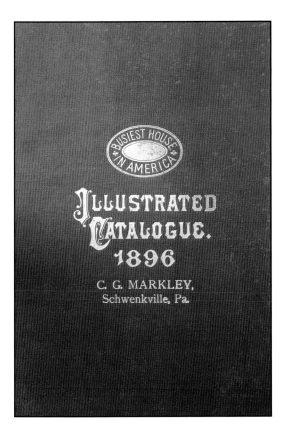

Cover of *Illustrated Catalogue*, 1896. C.G. Markley, Schwenkville, Pa., Busiest House in America.

Anonymous photograph of a Victorian interior, circa 1880.

Cabinet card of a young woman and child. The woman is wearing a comb in her hair, a brooch at her neck, and a watch chain from her bodice. Photo marked F. N. Hughes Cottage Studio, Mt. Kisco and Pawling, New York. Circa 1890 (the mutton-chop sleeves on the woman's dress were characteristic of the 1890s).

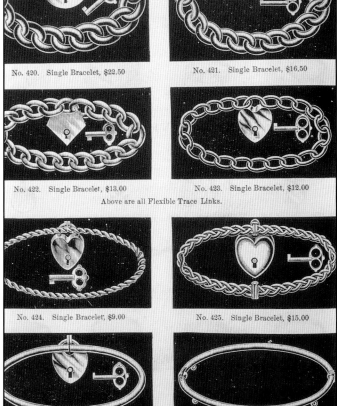

Bracelet with heart clasp. Circa 1890.

Illustrations of heart lock and key bracelets, p. 450.

While images of women as mothers and "guardians of the home" abound, the image of the erotic "Art Nouveau" woman also emerged during the 1890s. Idealized and sensual, liberated from constraints (notice the free-flowing hair and the frivolous nature of this young woman's pastime compared with the young, responsible, and corseted mother with a very restrained hairdo in the previous photograph). The chromolithograph is signed "Sarony." For additional information about Napoleon Sarony (who was also a noted photographer) see: http://www.library.upenn.edu/collections/rbm/keffer/sarony.html

Pencil drawing of a young woman by an artist identified as "E.V.S."

Another pencil drawing by the same artist.

Stereographic view of a woman who is taking a break from riding her bicycle and is not only showing her leg up to her knee, but she is also smoking a cigarette. She is flaunting conventionality at almost every turn! However, she is still wearing the high collared, long sleeved shirt and boater hat that were typical at the end of the nineteenth century.

5. Resting.

1890s-1910: White metal pencil with Stanhope ("In Memory of Stonehaven"), in the form of King Edward (2" x 1"). Silver clip in the garland style, with multicolored stones, prong and bezel set, marked "Sterling" (1 1/4" x 1"). Pressed aluminum and celluloid hair comb (2" x 5"). Black glass beads and faceted flowers on an oval brooch, (2" x 1 1/2", while this brooch is in a style popular during this era, it was made later). Two hearts, one in sterling silver and one in gold-plate with faux diamond chip (under 1/2").

Arts and Crafts style ring, with large oval amethyst (with inclusions) and two pearls, all bezel set, handmade, marked "14 K." (1" x 1 1/4"). Stick or scarf pins: one with a seed pearl prong-set on a gold design, one with a seed pearl set in the center of a delicately enameled four-leaf clover (marked "14 K." with a cross). Feather with a seed pearl, burnished and bloom gold finishes, marked "14" (2" x 1/4"). Gold retractable pen and pencil with repoussé image of a crew team sitting in a scull adorned with diamond chips, unmarked (2 3/4" x 1/4"). With gold pocket knife (blade marked J. A. Henckels), bloom and burnished gold (2 1/2" x 1/2"). Matching combs made of aluminum set with rhinestones, and faux tortoise shell (2" x 4"). Gold crescent pin with blue and pink enameled forget-me-nots and seed pearls (1" x 1/2"). Bar pin with rhinestones, marked "Sterling, Fishon, design patent pending" (3" x 1/2"). Vest pocket pencil with snake weaving in and out, marked "Sterling" with Edward Todd logo (3" x 1/2").

Note: Top center clip is in garland style but was made circa. 1930.

Photograph of a woman with a large hat, wearing two small brooches. Photograph marked H. Ginsberg, 82 Springfield Ave., Newark, New Jersey. 3 3/4" x 2 1/4". Newark was a jewelry manufacturing center in the 1800s.

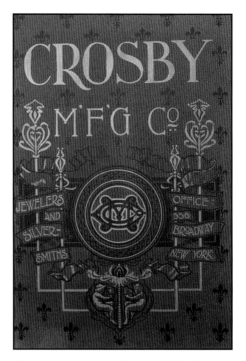

Cover of a jewelry catalogue published by *Crosby Manufacturing Company*, circa 1900.

Two young women wearing large hats and small brooches, from *The Delineator*, August, 1910 (page 133).

Page from *Crosby Manufacturing Company* catalogue, illustrating sterling silver and "chatton" [artificial diamond] brooches.

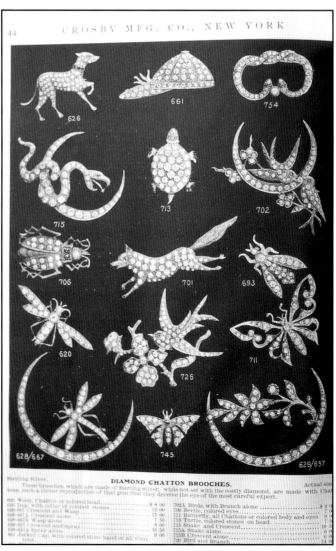

Sterling silver dog, set with
pastes. Unsigned, 1 1/2" x 3/4".
$175-$200.

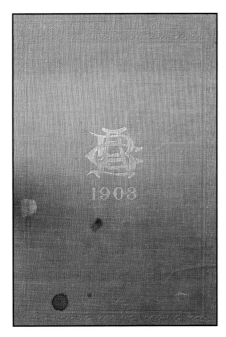

Cover of A. C. Becken Chicago Wholesale
Jeweler, 1903.

Color print of a woman holding her hat and golf bag triumphantly
over her head. Unsigned, early 1900s.

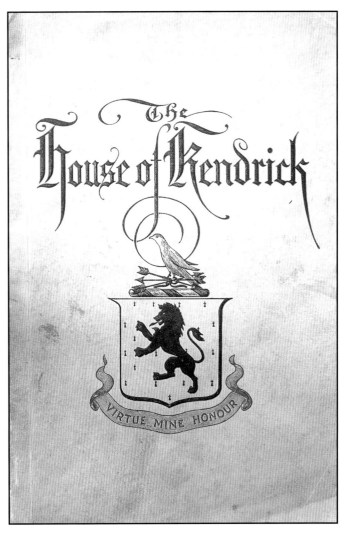

House of Kendrick Catalogue, Louisville, Kentucky, 1908. 10" x 6 1/2",
94 pages, $50-$75.

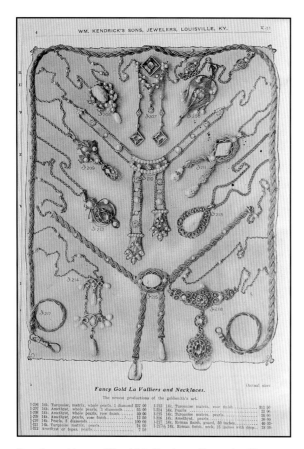

Page from *House of Kendrick Catalogue* illustrating "La Valliers" and necklaces, 1908.

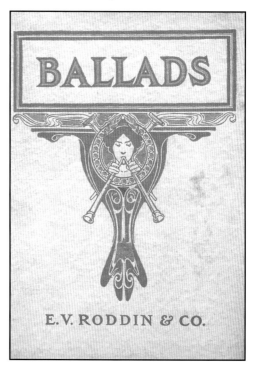

Catalogue, book of ballads published by *E. V. Roddin & Co.*, circa 1908. Included are pen and ink illustrations of fairies as well as photographs of the kinds of jewelry they offered for sale.

Illustration from *House of Kendrick Catalogue*.

Pen and ink drawing from E. V. Roddin catalogue.

Photograph of jewelry from E. V. Roddin catalogue.

Bracelet, signed "H & H" (Hamilton and Hamilton, Jr., in business from 1883 until 1922 in Providence, Rhode Island). Sterling silver and green glass beads, circa 1900. 7" x 1/2", $55-$75.

Postcard typical of the era, with symbols of friendship and good luck, 1906.

Brass hatpin holder in the shape of a ladies shoe, with an assortment of hatpins. Circa 1910, shoe 7" x 4", $75-$125. Focus on sterling silver golfer hat pin in center of photo.

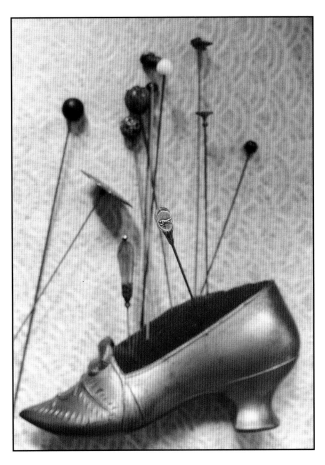

Daniel Low Catalog, 1910. By this date, catalogues are illustrated by photographs. 252 pages, paper cover, 9 1/2" x 6 1/2", $75-$100.

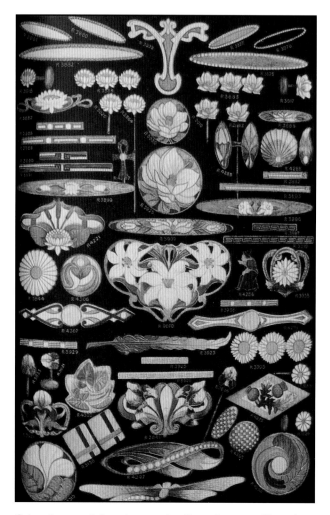

Color photograph from Low catalog illustrating enamel brooches.

Postcard from Saratoga Springs, New York, of the Adelphi Hotel. Circa 1910, published by Walter M. Stroup. An early automobile is shown in front of the now-historic hotel (which has been restored in its original Victorian splendor).

Postcard, tooled leather "Why the Devil Don't You Write?" 1909.

Postcard, tooled leather, with a man smoking a pipe: "I'm Thinking of You." The woman's face appears in the tobacco smoke. 1906.

1910-1930: *left to right, top to bottom:* Brass belt in the Egyptian style (26" x 1 1/2"). "American Women's Voluntary Services" from World War I, white metal and red, white, and blue enamel, marked "Robbins Co. Attleboro" (1" x 3/4"). Engraved money clip, telescoping pencil, rose and yellow gold, marked "Tiffany 14 K" (1 1/2" x 1 1/2"). Orange, burnt sienna, deep red, and green glass bead necklace with pharaohs heads, pyramids, and hieroglyphs, marked "Registered" (32" with 5" drop and pendants). Aluminum and celluloid hair comb with rhinestones (2 1/2" x 6"). Silver festoon necklace with blue stones and artificial seed pearls (16" x 1"). Fountain pen (eye dropper filled) in the shape of a mummy. Silver with multicolored enamel (3" x 1/2").

Unsigned fashion illustration, circa 1920. The world of fashion and style changed dramatically after World War I.

Anonymous photograph of a stylish young woman wearing a short skirt, in front of the most current mode of transportation. Circa 1920.

Watercolor of a woman wearing an elegant dress, with strands of pearls around her neck and one wrist, a gold and pearl cuff bracelet on the other, and long pearl earrings. Signed "Claire Enright, 1925."

Jade and silver earrings, circa 1920. These earrings would compliment the bobbed hairstyles of the '20s. *Courtesy of Bert Crosby.* N.P. (**N**o **P**rice)

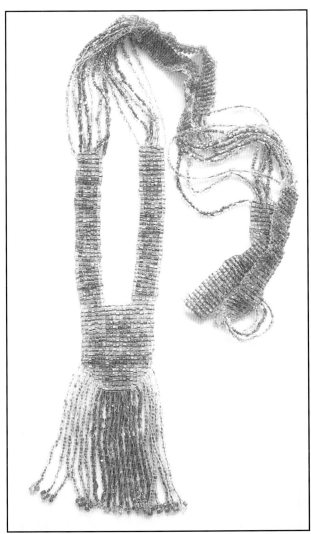

Sautior in fuchsia and clear beads, circa 1920. $75-$125.

Art Deco box in black and silver metal, with a stylized woman's face. $25-50.

Oil portrait of a pensive, blue eyed young woman with bobbed hair and a ring. Perhaps contemplating her engagement? Signed P. Marais, circa 1920.

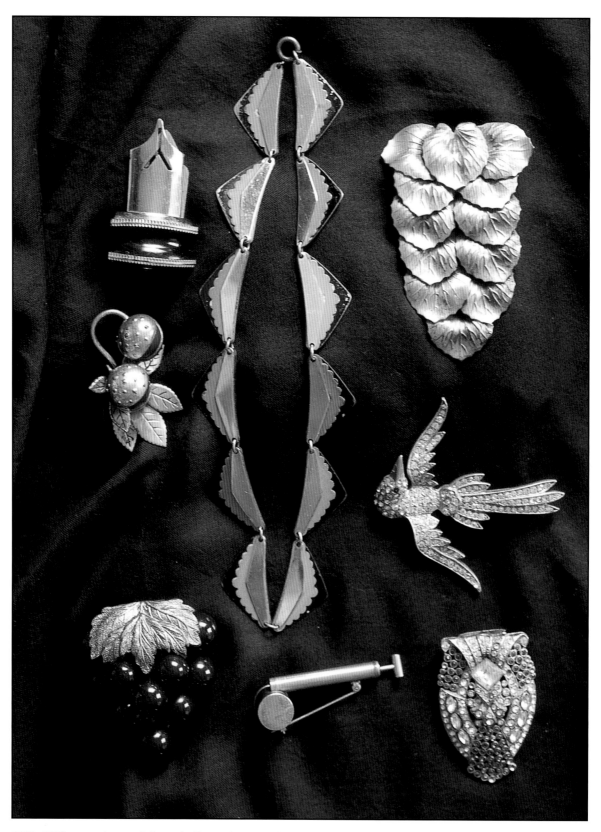

1920s-1930s: *top to bottom, left to right:* Dress clip made of brass and black enamel, in the form of a fountain pen nib (2" x 1"), unmarked. Brass and brown glass horse chestnut brooch (2" x 1"), unmarked. Brass and brown glass cluster of grapes, dress clip (2" x 2"), unmarked. Art Deco necklace, each segment consists of three layers: top layers are made of silver, center layers are brass pieces with scalloped edge enameled orange, and brass triangles made of brass with black enamel (15" x 3/4"), unmarked. Novelty perfume atomizer with working pump, made of brass (2" x 1/4"), unmarked. Dress clip with overlapping leaves, made of gilded brass (3 1/4" x 2"). Brooch in the shape of a flying bird, made of white metal, clear and red rhinestones, some enamel on beak (2 1/2" x 2 1/2"), unmarked. Dress clip (gilded nickel with white and garnet rhinestones, 2" x 1 1/4"), unmarked.

28

Chrysler ad, *Saturday Evening Post*, June 27, 1936.

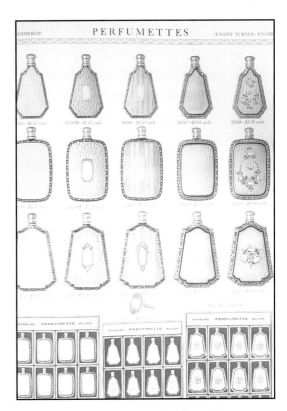

Illustration of silver and enamel perfumes from Webster catalogue.

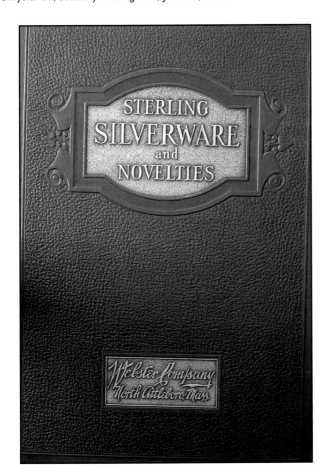

1930-1931 *Webster Sterling Silverware and Novelties* catalogue.

Sterling silver perfume bottle/pendant, 2" x 1 1/8",
engraved with initials "EDM." Circa 1930, $55-$75.

The 1934 *Becken Book* jewelry catalog.

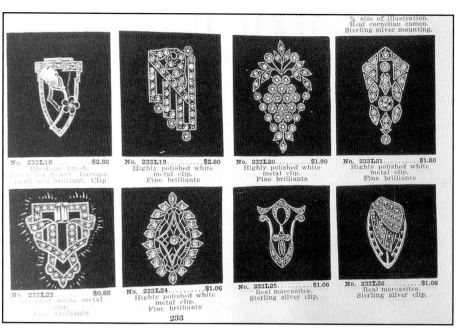

Illustration of dress clips from the *Becken Book*, page 233.

Within the catalog illustration:

¾ size of illustration.
Real cornelian cameo.
Sterling silver mounting.

No. 233L18.........$2.88
Rhodium finish.
Enameled flower. Baroque
pearl and brilliant. Clip

No. 233L19.........$2.60
Highly polished white
metal clip.
Fine brilliants

No. 233L20.........$1.90
Highly polished white
metal clip.
Fine brilliants

No. 233L21.........$1.80
Highly polished white
metal clip.
Fine brilliants

No. 233L23.........$0.88
Polished white metal
clip.
Fine brilliants

No. 233L24.........$1.06
Highly polished white
metal clip.
Fine brilliants

No. 233L25.........$1.06
Real marcasites.
Sterling silver clip.

No. 233L26.........$1.06
Real marcasites.
Sterling silver clip.

233

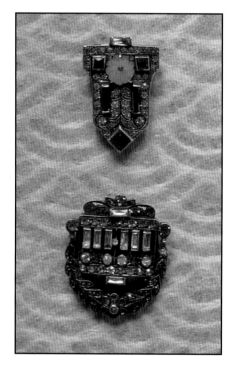

Sterling silver dress clips with multicolored stones. $175-250.

Photograph of a young woman wearing a dress with matching dress clips. Circa 1940. Unsigned.

Photograph from *Life Magazine*, April 13, 1942, page 106. In this photograph the model is exhibiting her patriotism by showing the patch on the seat of her pants. The article is entitled "Patches are Popular: War and Conservation Bring Them into the Open."

Modern Creations in Gold and Platinum catalogue from the late 1930s, early 1940s.

This photograph, from *Life Magazine*, April 27, 1942 (pages 98-99), illustrates the common luxuries made of metals that Americans could no longer purchase during the war.

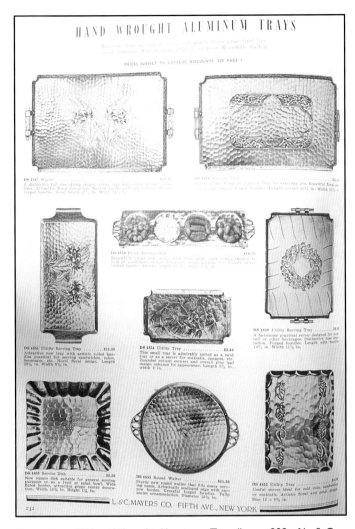

Illustration of "Hand Wrought Aluminum Trays," page 232 of L. & C. Mayers Co. Importers, Manufacturers, Distributors catalogue, 1942.

Still photos from 1940s movie: *Too Many Husbands* with Jean Arthur, Fred MacMurray, and Melvyn Douglas. *Photo by W. Swertfager Co.*

Still photo from *Earthbound* with Warner Baxter and Andrea Leeds. *Photo by W. Swertfager Co.*

Black and white photograph of Claudette Colbert signing autographs at Fort MacArthur, Army Canteen Service. *Photo by W. Swertfager Co.*

Opposing page:
1930-1940s: *left to right, top to bottom:* Aluminum ID bracelet, hand-machined and engraved with flowers and "Mother" (7 1/2" x 1/4"). Heavy brooch, marked "Sterling," stylized flowers and multicolored prong-set faux stones (3 1/2" x 2"). Brooch marked "Napier Sterling," with gold wash (2" x 2 1/2"). Heavy brooch marked "Sterling," with unusually shaped blue stone, prong-set emerald cut and round stones (3 1/2" x 2"), unmarked, but identical to brooch marked Mazer (Ball, *Costume Jewelers*, p. 107). Stylized ribbon brooch with green cabochon stones, marked "Sterling" (2 1/2" x 2"). Aluminum cuff bracelet, handmade (this bracelet is a remarkable combination of good design and excellent craftsmanship, the three layers, which are riveted together, are hand cut, filed, and engraved. The central flower spins like a propeller. A portion of the interior has the original black enamel paint, and is inscribed "Made from Jap [sic] Zero shot down Leyte 1944") (1 1/4" x 7"). Art Deco aluminum hat pins (approximately 2 1/4" x 1/2").

1940s fashion illustration "Lesson #5, 3 shades one color" Ada Conway for Miss Karasick. This drawing received an E- from the instructor.

Watercolor and pen and ink illustration of two young women in a city scene, circa 1940. Signed B. Lamb, 5" x 7".

1940s fashion silhouette, "Lesson #3" Ada Conway for Miss Karasick. This drawing earned a G+.

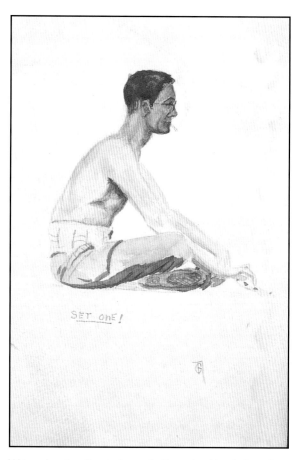

Watercolor of a sailor playing cards. From sketchbook drawn by George T. Heineman on board a ship and in India in 1945. Servicemen made jewelry out of aluminum for loved ones, a material generally unavailable for jewelry making due to the war.

Sterling silver charm bracelet with glass charms, circa 1940. $75-$125.

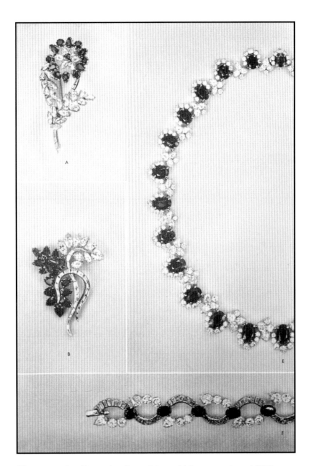

Photograph of jewelry from Harry Winston, circa 1950.

Cover of *Harry Winston Catalogue*.

Faux sapphire and diamond demi-parure in original box.
$125-$150.

1950s: *left to right, top to bottom:* Gilded collar, with cabochon turquoise, lapis lazuli, sapphire blue enamel, and pearls (14" x 1 1/2"), unmarked, but with extraordinary workmanship. (Each turquoise has a different pattern, each backed with a stamped filigree and wire support. Jump links are serrated, cloisonné enamel matches lapis cabochons, each simulated pearl is bezel set.) "Miriam Haskell" (marked on oval tag at clasp) white pâte de verre and gilded brass filigree necklace (18" with pendant 2 1/2" x 1 1/2"). Copper necklace in the shape of stylized calla lilies, marked "Morely-Crimi Hand Wrought" (17" x 1/4"). Faux pearl, rhinestone, burnished gold (plated) earrings, marked "Eugene" (1 1/4" x 1 1/4"). Cuff bracelet, marked "Rebajes," made of copper (2" x 6 1/2"). Aluminum bracelet in the daisy pattern, marked "Wendell August Forge 3 80" (1 1/2" x 6 1/2").

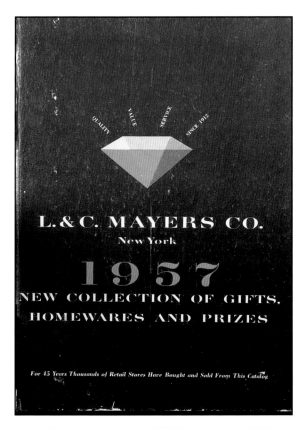

L. & C. Mayers Co. New York 1957 New Collection of Gifts, Homewares and Prizes.

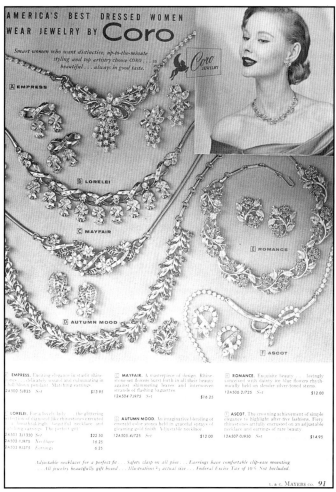

Illustration (from Mayers catalog) of Coro jewelry, page 91.

Anonymous painting, circa 1955.

Illustration of models wearing sweater sets, page 248.

Patti Criore, 11" x 14". "Evening Gown: Fabric-Skirt of chiffon over silk organza. Color—Bodice is paved with black, white & lavender paillettes. Skirt is lavender."

Pop-beads were popular throughout the 1950s and into the 1960s. $5-$10 a strand.

Ink and beaded image of a woman wearing a long skirt and bonnet, holding an umbrella. Those of us growing up in the Fifties remember all the cowboy shows on TV, and the arts and crafts projects that we worked on when we weren't watching television.

Patti Criore, 11" x 14". "Negligee: Color—Yellow & white. Fabric—Nylon tricot, velvet trims. Detail—Bodice has petals which are partly attached & stick up from top center of flowers and ties are velvet."

1950s-1960s: *left to right, top to bottom:* Coral colored pâte de verre beads, burnished gold morning glory on stamped filigree, marked "Miriam Haskell" on hasp (28" with 2 1/2" x 3" pendant), with matching earrings. Faux baroque pearls, marked "Miriam Haskell." Star-shaped pin, marked "Corocraft ©" with cultured pearl and marcasite, gold and silver washes on textured base. Brooch in the form of a moth, with faux baroque pearl body, clear and green rhinestones, gold wash, en tremblant (2" x 1 1/2"), marked "Pauline Rader." Renaissance revival hinged bracelet with gold and silver washes, green chrysoprase cabochon, faux rubies, emeralds, amethysts, coral, rubies, rhinestones, marked "KJL ©" (Kenneth Jay Lane) (3/4" x 6 1/2").

The '60s: flower power and bubble rings ... $5-$25.

Cover of *The Saturday Evening Post*, November 30, 1968. For those of us who remember when the TV show "Laugh In" was first broadcast, this cover brings back memories of staying home every Monday night so we wouldn't miss any of the outrageously funny episodes. There were no VCR's then, and if you missed a show you'd have to wait for the summer reruns. This magazine also carries an article about a daytime soap opera entitled "Dark Shadows," the first and probably only soap opera about a vampire, which was also new and terribly popular in 1968.

In addition to the visual timeline described above, I've also included a series of photographs showing how jewelry that is based on a certain theme (in this case, insects) changes and evolves between 1860 and 1960. Some of the insect jewelry is rendered realistically, and some is stylized. I wish I had been able to find an example of the extremely novel style that appeared briefly at the close of the nineteenth century, in which actual insects were either attached to tiny chains or worn in little cages that dangled from a woman's earlobes. Imagine the effect of lightening bugs flashing their mating signals against the lily white neck of a late Victorian woman! The fact that bug jewelry has its own incarnation each generation is, I think, fascinating. Butterflies, bees, flies, ladybugs, even a mosquito or two, have graced many a bodice.

Collections Shared

Two friends generously offered to share collections of jewelry that they inherited. While they are not major groupings as compared to the collections shown in exhibits like "Masterpieces of American Jewelry" (American Folk Art Museum) or the Castellani show (Bard Graduate Center), they are significant to the owners. It is interesting to see, for example, an early twentieth century photograph of a young woman wearing a pin that is still in pristine condition nearly one hundred years later. It is even more interesting to know the descendent, and to hear her describe the jewelry that has been passed down from one generation to another.

The images and the text in this book follow a rather eclectic path. It seems to me that learning is not neat and tidy, and that one of the great pleasures of education is synthesis. Serendipity plays a part, too, I believe. So the path that I hope to lead you on wanders a bit and takes an occasional shortcut and, well, more often follows the longer, more scenic route. The timelines provide an important context, as this book is not only non-chronological but it is also not structured like any other jewelry book I've read. And

that, my dear reader, is the point!

Jewelry Camp

Last summer, I finally had the chance to participate in an absolutely wonderful program, affectionately known as "Jewelry Camp." The official title, "Joyce Jonas & Associates, Inc. Annual Antique and Period Jewelry and Gemstone Conference" sounds appropriately serious, as this is an intense program. But it is Jewelry Camp! The presenters are knowledgeable, the faculty is gifted, the campers—ah, students, are enthusiastic and curious. Where else can you hear a presentation by Judy Rudoe (from the British Museum, author of several books on Cartier), have lunch with Christie Romero (author of three editions of *Warman's Jewelry*) before you attend her marvelous workshop on material identification (and yes, she made sure that I didn't breathe any toxic fumes), attend a presentation by Geza Von Hapsburg (in which he talks about the jewelry his family once owned), and party, I mean study, until early morning with jewelry aficionados who will become great friends? The next day, you hear Janet Zapata speak about the upcoming Seaman Schepps exhibit and speak with Lynn Levenberg about an incredible collection of jewelry that she curates (you just might meet the collector she works for, but that is a secret). You have dinner with some of the most interesting, supportive people you will ever meet, and, uh, study again well into the night. Laura Hisersote and her talented son, Jared, demonstrate through their work with micro mosaics that both remarkable craftsmanship and dedication to the arts live on. You meet one of America's premiere jewelers, you ask questions of everyone who's ever been on the "Roadshow," and you are awed by the entire production.

If you want to study the history of jewelry, this program is a must. It is remarkable how much you can learn in seven very busy days!

Flea Markets

You will never know what you will find when you go to a flea market. Sometimes, nothing. Other times, you will find tantalizing bits and pieces that will make the quest interesting. Then there are times when you find amazing treasures. A few weeks ago I was on my way out of a market after spending about four unproductive hours (well, looking is always a learning experience, so it wasn't totally fruitless. It was also the first Sunday in what seemed like ten years that the sun was actually shining.) and I backtracked across an aisle I had seen earlier. A Japanese lacquer tray caught my eye. When I asked the vendor about it, he said that he had several additional pieces from the same box lot and that if I was interested to look back by his van. What I found was more lacquer ware: boxes, trays, bowls, etc., some Japanese, some Chinese, some old, and some early nineteenth century. Not only were the pieces beautiful, but they were all labeled "Stamford Auction Gallery, from the Estate of Louise Nevelson."

Louise Nevelson was a major twentieth century sculptor and a flamboyant, passionate woman. It was thrilling to discover that one of the boxes was filled with safety pins, because Nevelson was known to create an outfit by draping herself in fabric and safety-pinning it together. Her choices in jewelry were avant garde, and I am pleased that I was given permission to include a photograph of one of the pieces she owned in this book.

Flea markets are great places to find parts, stones, old books (I found several that were once owned by Napier Company), etc. In other words, bits and pieces of history, parts of a puzzle that may take years to complete. It is possible to find molds that were used for casting, unfinished jewelry, even prototypes of articles that never made it into production. You never know what will turn up!

Found in a flea market in Connecticut, these are discarded masters from a jewelry manufacturer. Molds would be made from these metal originals (with metal attached to the sprue, which is the channel melted metal is poured into during the casting process).

Masters for making molds for casting rings, with design drawings for the rings. The master would be made of metal the and mold would be cast from it. Whenever the mold became worn and unusable, a new mold was made from the master.

Mold and masters for casting jewelry.

A variety of stones found at a flea market. It is helpful to collect stones like these — one never knows when they will come in handy for a repair.

Masters for a variety of rings (and envelopes for identification).

More stones.

The colors and shapes are fascinating.

Metal jewelry findings, die stamped and cut. Filigree, medallions, etc. Also found in a Connecticut flea market. These are the pre-fabricated components that are used to construct jewelry.

Colorful variety of glass, pâte de verre, and natural gems that were used by a jewelry manufacturer. Mid-twentieth century.

Jewelry findings of various non-precious metals. Some of these would have been plated when they were used in jewelry.

Sample panel with an assortment of die-stamped metal strips used in jewelry making. Late nineteenth, early twentieth century.

Unfinished charm bracelet, with prototype components.

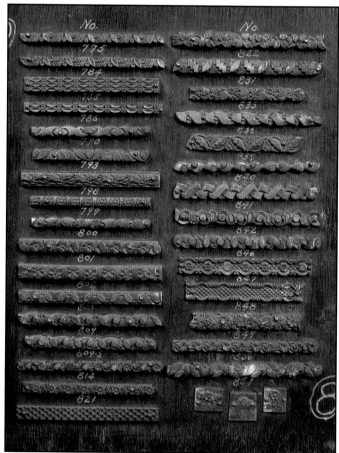

Sample panel from the same company.

Steel dies for jewelry making.

Steel die for embossing a badge, circa 1900. Flea markets are a great place to find objects that are interesting historically but not particularly valuable monetarily.

Steel die for "Salem Eng." Crossed cannons (probably used to create a medal). Die stamping required precise molds and heavy duty equipment. This die is made of steel, weighs about ten pounds, and would withstand the pressure of the punch being hammered into it while the metal was die-stamped.

Metal parts for jewelry.

The Quest

*T*o adorn oneself with jewelry is distinctly human. It reflects the hopes and dreams of the people of an era. It demonstrates the values, the emphasis, the inventions, and the role of individuals within the society. It reflects how people live, how they spend their time and their money, how they solve problems, how they determine value, how they allocate resources, how they express themselves, and how they envision the future. To see how our ancestors who lived between 1860 and 1960 addressed the dilemma of creating enough jewelry to satisfy everyone while still maintaining its value is a fascinating study. By observing trends and being able to discern when certain things that were once novel, but have lost their novelty, popularity or utility become rare, is an important skill for a collector. For example, when jewelry was made of black hard rubber initially, it was a novelty that was an affordable substitute for Whitby jet. Because it was black, it served well as mourning jewelry, which was prevalent at the time of its invention both because of Queen Victoria's extended mourning for Prince Albert and, in America, because of the numbers of men killed in the Civil War. Vulcanite jewelry was worn for a period of about ten years before it fell out of popular favor, and never regained its popularity. Hence, when other materials supplanted it, and when black hard rubber was no longer a novelty, jewelry made of it was discarded. The material alone would not have been reason enough to save it, it oxidized and sometimes developed a greenish-brown surface; it became brittle and was thrown away. Now, nearly one hundred forty years later, it is relatively rare, and hard enough to find in good condition to become fairly valuable.

In this book, there are certainly photographs of jewelry made of gold and silver and set with precious stones. Also included, though, are photographs of jewelry made of black hard rubber (vulcanite or ebonite), aluminum, hair, glass (strass, pâte de verre, rhinestone, crystal, etc.), and plastics, jewelry that while not made of a precious metal has become valuable none-the-less. Simple antique gold bracelets can sell for under $200. However, certain costume jewelry can sell for far more, even though it may be made of gilded base metal rather than gold. Vulcanite bracelets can sell for more, if they are unusual and in excellent condition. Jewelry made from alternative materials can be highly collectible and expensive. Recently, at the Triple Pier Antiques Show in New York City, I saw a striking necklace that had bakelite pens, pencils, and other teacher paraphernalia suspended from a bakelite chain. It seemed as if it had been custom made for me, until I asked the price: $1,200! Bakelite jewelry has clearly become established, and is a perfect example of jewelry that's made of a non-precious material that's valuable nevertheless. But there are still good buys out there, still avenues to be explored.

One collector calls those of us who are seeking to find collectibles that haven't become collectible yet "bargain hunters." I'd rather see myself as a trendsetter, but perhaps that's only my ego speaking. It is challenging, I think, to learn about what was created and what was worn in the past, then to scour flea markets, antiques shows, and the internet to see what's available in quantities and what isn't, and to find the right balance between what's rare and what's totally unavailable. It's important to reassess what we consider common, or common knowledge, and to look at materials and definitions as they were considered when they were new. Costume jewelry is a good example of that. By the time I was a teenager, costume jewelry was the term that was used for any and every form of cheap bauble. It meant fake, artificial, fraudulent, impermanent, and either disgustingly gaudy or unforgivably conservative. Yet, by reassessing my perception of that phrase and by understanding it in context of the era in which it originated, I now know that there are distinct differences between cheap, mass-produced "fake" jewelry and real, well-designed (and often handmade or hand-assembled) costume jewelry.

When I started this book, I owned two pieces of what I would now categorize as costume jewelry: a pair of unmarked earrings with cabochon stones and gilded metal fringe and a very handsome brooch that is marked "Mazer." The earrings and the brooch are very well made, and I am sure I entertained some fantasies of having discovered real treasures in a thrift shop in Saratoga Springs and in my great-aunt's jewelry box. It was confusing because I knew the stones weren't real and I knew that the metals would most likely be marked if they were gold, silver, or platinum (and they were not marked). Yet the jewelry had a certain authenticity to it that the kind of "costume jewelry" I was then familiar with did not have. Now, after seeing many examples of high quality, expensive costume jewelry I realize that these pieces of jewelry are utterly unlike what I had seen so much of before. There is a world of difference between the trinkets I used to see at Woolworth's in the 1960s and the kind of costume jewelry that was sold at high end stores. It did seem real because it was really well made.

There are several categories that jewelry can fall into. There are one-of-a-kind pieces, there are pieces signed by major jewelers (in jewelry, the term generally used for marked pieces is "signed" even if the example is only stamped, rather than actually signed, with the maker's name). There is fine (as well as costume) jewelry that is manufactured in bulk, mass-produced, and there are one-of-a-kind pieces of costume jewelry.

Because of this book, I've read biographies of people as diverse as Charles Goodyear and Louise Nevelson (although they certainly had one thing in common: a personal vision and the immense determination to bring that vision into reality). Charles Goodyear invented vulcanite, of which fascinating jewelry was made during the mid-nineteenth century. Louise Nevelson, twentieth century American sculptor, loved to adorn herself with unusual jewelry. I listen to the news differently (last week, in broad daylight, a thief used his tools to cut into a jewelry store in downtown Greenwich, Connecticut, and managed to steal over $12,000 worth of jewelry while a policeman directed traffic nearby). I read the paper with new interest (jewelers in NYC allegedly cast gold into such mundane items as hammers so it could be exported undetected to South America, in an effort to circumvent the legal system in its mission to track down money made through illicit drug trade).

It's been an eclectic search, and I've found myself learning more about Elvis Presley, Coco Chanel, Miriam Haskell, paintings at the Metropolitan Museum of Art, the history of aluminum, famous people who collect jewelry, manufacturing, trade unionism in the jewelry business, security, Bohemia (is it a coincidence that it is considered so very Bohemian to wear beads?), ancient Egypt, archeological discoveries, fashion, social movements, the history of photography, chromolithography, several wars, inventions, terminology, and the influence of Japanese culture on American decorative arts.

Connections come in surprising packages, as when I was reading Bram Stoker's *Dracula* and discovered that the name of the seaside town in which the story begins (where lovely, gentle Lucy is first bitten) is none other than Whitby. The evil canine beast leaps out of the ship at the pier in Whitby Harbor. Whitby is the source of a shiny, dense, coal-like material known as Whitby jet, which was used extensively in the manufacture of mourning jewelry. I doubt Stoker's choice of this particular English town was coincidental.

I look at paintings differently, and now notice the jewelry the individual wore when he or she sat for a portrait. I not only notice jewelry that other people are wearing, but it has become evident to me that other people also notice jewelry. I pay attention to the jewelry worn by actors and actresses in movies, I look to see the loaner pieces worn by Academy Awards winners, I regret all the opportunities I missed and all the times I passed by boxes of jewelry at flea markets and tag sales.

I found myself learning more about friends and colleagues. One of my dear friends, now an octogenarian, is the son of a Bohemian immigrant who designed and made jewelry for William Scheer, who provided jewelry for Cartier and Van Cleef and Arpels. One colleague, now an official antiques dealer as well as a terrific Spanish teacher, inspired me by wearing colorful bakelite pins on her jacket lapel. Another creative friend wears her antique pins and brooches clustered together in such an unusual way as to make it intriguing to see how she'll compose her next grouping. One friend, also a wonderful language teacher, fell in love with a gorgeous ring and put it on lay-away, tutoring until she had enough extra cash to wear the ring home. A friend shared the photograph of her mother as a child, wearing the very same gold bar pins that she inherited and let me photograph. The wife of another colleague has the aluminum bracelet her father made for her mother when he was serving overseas in World War II. A husband lovingly told stories about his wife's great aunt, whom she had inherited jewelry from. I found myself looking at the charm bracelet my grandmother wore with new insight. In other words, jewelry has not only been an intellectual study, but a personal one as well.

The down side, of course, is time. Despite how it appeared to one of my daughters when she was young, I don't just sit down at the computer and "all of a sudden a book is done." It takes time to read, to research, to track down clues, to visit shows, museums, libraries, to digest information, and to put it together in such a way that others will find it, hopefully, useful and entertaining. My friends and family have been pretty understanding and many of my colleagues supportive. This book covers a far greater spectrum than my other books, and it took me a while to narrow my focus enough to produce a book that has a common thread while at the same time examining the different kinds of jewelry that were available to the typical American between 1860 and 1960.

My art students were enthusiastic when I shared some tidbit about the history of jewelry, and when I showed them things I had discovered at the flea market (like the Japanese lacquer box that Louise Nevelson kept trinkets in, that still smells like her perfume when you open it). Hopefully, now when my students ask me what I did over my summer break, I will be able to say I finished writing a book on jewelry.

Books and Stories

*F*or those who are interested in pursuing additional information, I am recommending books at the end of each section. The bibliography is extensive, and lists many more books than are noted in each chapter. It is my hope that it will provide readers with information that will assist them as they become more involved in the study of jewelry. Since this book covers not only the spectrum of types of jewelry that were worn by Americans between 1860-1960, but also what was going on in America during that century, the bibliography also includes biographies, histories, and technical references. The dates of publication span almost 140 years, from the 1860s to 2005. The reader should have the opportunity to see how events, styles, etc., were perceived when they were current as well as how they have been interpreted subsequent to the passage of time. It is interesting to see the various revivals of certain styles. It is fascinating to compare what the United States was like in the mid-1860s, during the Civil War, to the mid-1960s (during the war in Vietnam). It is remarkable to contrast the kinds of dresses women were wearing in 1910 to the dresses they were wearing in the 1920s. Coco Chanel, for example, grew up wearing ankle length skirts with tiny waists but was designing dresses in what we would call the flapper style by 1926 (these dresses fell straight from the shoulder to the knee, not only de-emphasizing the waist and bust but exposing the leg).

Antiques dealers were wonderfully helpful. Some have incredible taste and extensive knowledge. I've learned a great deal from many of them.

This book is going to be much more anecdotal than the others books I've written, and it will be written through my personal point of view. I've met interesting people, heard interesting stories, and realize now that the lore of jewelry is one of the things that make it such a fascinating study. There are excellent books on jewelry, and I would encourage the reader to expand his or her library to include as many of these books as possible. However, I also realize that it is a bit easier to have as much information as possible in one source, so I am including history as well as technical information. This is not the most standard scholarly approach and I ask forgiveness (in advance) of those who taught me to write in the third person. I am writing to each of you who read this book, and I am writing as if we may meet at a flea market or tag sale and have a conversation, and perhaps we shall.

There are finds out there, still wonderful discoveries to be made. It seems, though, that it gets harder to find things after a while, as your standards generally become higher and you become less willing to take chances and more likely strive to buy only the best. It's probable that after years of collecting, you'll go to the flea markets intent on finding something, only to discover that what's out there is junk, outright garbage, stuff you'd put by the side of the road on bulk pickup day. You remember what it's like to make brilliant discoveries, the diamond in the rough, the whatever that's worth a fortune but for which you had to pay only a few dollars. We remember, back in the old days, how the markets were filled with really old things, things that could be honestly called antiques. Victorian silver was really cheap because it was plentiful and, after all, who wanted it? But wait, didn't I just finish writing a book on Victorian silver, and didn't I see how difficult it is to find examples? When did that happen?

When many of us started out, whatever we were looking for was probably pretty available. The generation ahead of us laughed at our purchases (I recall being virtually thrown out of antiques shows because all I was looking for were fountain pens and, good heavens, did the mature dealer look down his or her very aristocratic nose at me!). I remember going to country auctions were there were real rope beds, where my parents bought genuine antique chairs just so we could sit down for the day. There were buffalo robes galore (dusty old things! Until I found out that one of my brother's friends found an actual Native American painting on the underside of one, I would never have wanted to bring a shaggy, moth eaten lap robe into the house), lap desks with the original contents, trunks full of nineteenth century dresses, entire houses filled with generations worth of possessions … these were all fairly common sights and we took it for granted. Things have changed, and that's just the way it is! We need to change, too, and look for things that may be readily available today but not tomorrow (as in "here today, gone tomorrow").

While access to an extensive library is essential (the bibliography in this book should be helpful), many questions will remain unanswered if one refers only to what's currently in print. It is imperative to have an understanding of styles, techniques, known makers, materials, trends … and it is equally important to have a sense of history. Knowing that materials like aluminum were in short supply during World War II makes it easier to understand why little commercial jewelry was made of it during that era, and why costume jewelry was fabricated of sterling silver (which was not useful in the war effort). Knowing that aluminum jewelry created during the Second World War was largely made by hand, by soldiers and sailors from bits and pieces of weapons and airplanes, makes the few pieces that exist today all the more precious. But that's not usually the kind of information you'll find in print (I am still looking for descriptions of soldiers working aluminum, and expect that it is more likely that I will find something in a contemporary journal or letter than a book).

The challenge is to try to find out what's not going to be common tomorrow. To see what's out there and recognize things that in a few years will be in short supply. It helps to be able to approach the field, if at all possible, like we did in the beginning (when we were novices) and look for things that other people may currently disdain. Aluminum jewelry would be an example. I remember seeing aluminum jewelry fairly often in the past, but it is becoming increasingly difficult to find today.

A collector must be willing to make personal connections between not only the dealers and other collectors, but between him or herself and the objects he or she collects. The collector must be able and willing to create a unique and individual synthesis of what he or she sees at antiques shows or flea markets. The collector must be able to follow leads, follow his or her heart, and learn to follow where the collection leads.

Follow Your Heart

*S*peaking of the heart, that wonderful shape could well inspire a collection. Perhaps the collection begins with an inherited charm bracelet, one that has names and birth dates engraved on hearts and disks. That could entice the collector, perhaps, to seek out other simple heart-shaped charms, but from an earlier era. Knowing that most collectors challenge themselves by seeking more unusual examples, a gold heart with red enamel pierced by a miniscule mechanical pencil could be the next addition to the collection. Again, as collectors generally aspire to find better and better specimens of whatever they collect, the level of challenge tends to increase, and someone who once looked for simple, unmarked heart charms may find oneself falling in love with other jewelry related to the topic. A person could begin to see hearts not just as charms, but as figural Victorian pencils, lockets and coin cases, and eventually start collecting Unger Brother jewelry embellished with cupids and other imagery specific to the theme. Looking for jewelry that's heart shaped may motivate the collector to learn more about the origin of the imagery. According to Diane Ackerman (page 146 of *A Natural History of Love*) the heart may be used as a symbol of love because "the heart is vital to being alive…and so is love." But while that describes one reason why the heart is used as a symbol of love, it doesn't explain how the actual heart shape evolved. Some theorize that the shape was created before there was a true understanding of what a human heart looked like (Howstuffworks: How Valentines Day works http://ads.specificpop.com/pop_code;gid=17, pid=90,bid=591). www.heartsmith.com/heart History.html

It's also possible that the shape was not a stylized version of a human heart, but rather was derived from the silhouette of female pelvic bones (hence the phallic symbolism of the arrow which pierces it). A collector may fall for a heart-shaped locket, a gun-metal coin case in the shape of a heart, a sterling silver pin from the mid-twentieth century with a key piercing a heart…to keys that are actually a pen, pencil and pen-knife attached to a heart- shaped chatelaine, to nineteenth century gold and silver pencils shaped like keys, to twentieth century, key-shaped signed costume jewelry… a collector might then develop an interest in jewelry with original tags, which could pique ones interest in jewelry in original packaging…all of a sudden the collector wants to learn about Elvis Presley and Elvis Presley Enterprises, which reminds the collector of his or her interest in playing guitar as a teenager, then of other pastimes that kept the young collector safely occupied, like bowling for example…

The ability to synthesize tends to be trait collectors share (or perhaps we just never passed the "sorting" stage in our early childhood development!).

Try to find something that is well made, with enough examples available to keep you interested, but an item where there aren't so many that there is no challenge.

Establish a niche. Don't be afraid to be the only person who is crazy enough to collect a certain kind of item, or jewelry of a certain style or theme. Have confidence in yourself and look for objects that you personally find intriguing. You may be teased at the outset and you may find few examples of whatever it is you're looking for initially. But influential collectors are rarely those who follow trends, but rather are more likely to be those who set trends. Look carefully at what's available and what's not being collected now. A few years ago, nobody wanted jewelry made of vulcanized rubber. Now it's difficult to find examples under $100. What kinds of things are available now that won't be in a few years? Look ahead. Which trends will affect what's in the market? Would it be smart to buy cigarette holders now, in light of the fact that fewer and fewer establishments allow smoking on their premises or in light of the fact that very few people who are alive today have ever seen someone using one? There are collapsible cigarette holders that fit in tiny cases that hang as charms from necklaces or bracelets.

Speaking of charms, there are all sorts of miniatures that can be assembled in masses or worn individually, in silver or gold. There are examples as simple as one that has hearts and disks engraved with the names and birth dates of grandchildren, or as complex and expensive as the ones worn by Elizabeth Taylor (see her book, *My Love Affair With Jewelry*). Charms can be collected by or for a child (my daughters used to look for them when they accompanied me to flea markets). They can initiate a new collector to the selection process. For relatively little money a collector can find examples of charms that have personal, symbolic meaning, and that may lead a new collector to search for other pieces in the same theme. In the past few years, charm bracelets have become popular again and there are at least two books that will be of interest to a charm collector.

Recommended Reading

Jade Albert, Ki Hackney. *The Charm of Charms.*

Joanne Schwartz. *Charms and Charm Bracelets: The Complete Guide.*

Tracy Zabar. *Charmed Bracelets.*

Adding a "signed" piece of costume jewelry to ones collection could inspire a person to start seeking additional signed pieces, or may lead the collector to discover examples that are not actually marked but that are identifiable by original packaging, labels, or tags. The jointed fish pendant was made by Napier (http://www.cooljools.com/Hall_of_Fame.htm) and still has its original tag. A charm bracelet with symbols for man, woman, infinity, etc. (all those popular sixties themes) is still attached to its original packaging, which informs us that this "Ben Casey" (as portrayed by Vincent Edwards, pictured on the right) charm bracelet was produced in 1962 by Bing Crosby Productions. Without the packaging, there would be no way to know any of this information, as the bracelet is not marked. The same is true of the white metal and bakelite charm bracelet produced by Elvis Presley Enterprises. Collecting jewelry is fun, it's an adventure, it's an opportunity to explore, to make connections, to learn about history and culture. It's amazing how much of this history is still at our fingertips. We (well, some of us) think of jewelry made in the 1950s as relatively new, yet it's already been a half century since it was created. It's actually from another century altogether, another millennium!

If a certain style becomes popular, look towards the origins of the trend. Turquoise jewelry may be au currant and relatively costly when purchased in jewelry or department stores, but there may be some magnificent older pieces that can be purchased for half the price at a flea market. Festoon necklaces (chains with trinkets, beads, and/or set stones dangling from them) have been going in and out of style for centuries, and you may be able to find one that's one hundred years old and made of sterling silver and semi-precious stones for the same price as a new one that's made of base metal and plastic. The coral jewelry that's being sold in high-end department stores may be copied from a natural strand that you found in your grandmother's jewelry box, and the earrings may be replicas of the ones you saw in an antiques shop. We are living in an exciting time, as far as fashion and jewelry are concerned. Jewelry today is often bold and colorful, and it seems that people are more confident wearing interesting pieces. Costume jewelry is more appealing than it has been in a long time, I think, and magazine editors are doing a great job of showing the many varieties in a variety of price ranges (thanks to people like Penny Prodow and Marion Fasel for their column in *InStyle* magazine).

Know your stuff! Examine things carefully to learn as much as you can while you're out in the field. Notice what makes items similar, what makes them unique. Keep an open mind because there are lots of things that we don't know, despite what we think we know, that we won't learn unless we listen. Dealers often have many years of experience and will be willing to offer advice and suggestions if you take the time to consult with them. You will read that you should see and handle as much jewelry as possible, and that is good advice.

Decide what style of collecting works best for you. Do you want only the best examples of expensive jewelry, in pristine condition? Are you in the market for jewelry to wear to work, signature pieces to wear on the lapel of your jacket? Do you want to find lots of examples while you're out at the flea markets and estate sales or do you want to find very few pieces at high-end antiques shows or through experienced dealers? Do you want your collection to grow quickly or do you want to spend years amassing your collection?

Jewelry can be collected by material (silver, gold, glass, aluminum, bakelite, plastic, micro mosaic, diamond, turquoise, vulcanite, gutta-percha, silver plate, mixed metals, etc.), era (Victorian, Edwardian, Art Nouveau, Art Deco, and so on), purpose (necklaces, earrings, rings, chains, pencils, pens...), or subject matter (for someone who sells cell phones, brooches in the form of old-fashioned telephones may be a perfect idea). Policitcal buttons, ribbons that were worn in parades, cuff links, scarf pins, posy holders, jewelry catalogs, advertising, ephemera, letter heads, jewelry casks or boxes, silver pins that are in the shape of feathers or quills, figurals (jewelry that is in the shape of a recognizable object—an orchid for example), affordable (you can find great buys if you are willing to search), jewelry that may be common today, but gone tomorrow (how long do we think belly button rings will be in style?); there are endless possibilities.

Collections may span many eras and still have certain characteristics that relate one piece to another. As you look through this book, notice how flowers (for example) have been depicted in different eras. Some flowers are rendered realistically, while others are stylized. Some are made of precious metals, some of plastic. There are bold flowers and dainty ones. A collection of jeweled corsages would be fun to assemble and great to wear.

If you allow yourself to look beyond what you are accustomed to collecting, you may find something that you wouldn't notice otherwise. This inexpensive pin is a beauty, and I almost passed it by because it was plated and not sterling silver.

Charm bracelet, started in 1952. Sterling silver. $50-$125. The theme for a collection may originate when a collector-to-be inherits a piece of jewelry. This can act as a catalyst, as the individual may start to do research about the inherited jewelry and may seek out other examples. (The person whose name is engraved on the first silver heart was born in 1952, and was sixteen when Rowan and Martin were spoofing "Free love is cheap at half the price" or Goldie Hawn was holding a sign indicating that "Virtue is its own punishment" (*Post*, 1968, page 33).

Tiny silver and rolled gold hearts, 1880-1910. $15-$25. A novice collector may want to start small, or a collector may want to suggest relatively inexpensive items that children who accompany a parent to flea markets, etc., can begin collecting.

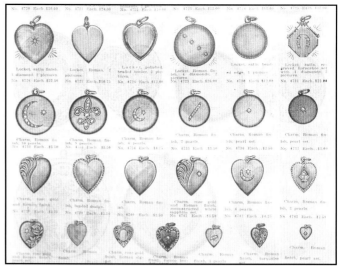

Illustration of heart lockets from *General Illustrated Catalogue* of the Fort Dearborn Watch and Clock Co., page 153 (circa 1890). Once a collection is established, it's helpful to see the range of objects that were created during a particular period. It helps to know what to look for.

Gold heart with engine-turned pattern under red enamel (basse taille) pierced by a tiny gold pencil in the shape of an arrow. Circa 1870, $650-$775. If a collector is open minded, he or she may find enormous variations on a particular theme. Although the red heart isn't itself terribly unusual, the fact that it houses an incredibly small pencil makes it rare.

Postcard, circa 1890, "From a faithful friend with love sincere." Studying ephemera enhances our understanding of the culture that produced the objects.

Sterling silver locket in the shape of a heart, with repoussé flowers. *Courtesy of Rachel Marks Antiques.* $375-$450.

Lucite hearts (3/4" x 3/4") on sterling silver chain (16"). Circa 1940, $250-$275.

Gun-metal coin case in the shape of a heart, circa 1890. $175-$275.

"Coro" heart with wings pin, sterling silver with gold overlay, amethyst glass stones. Circa 1940, 3 1/4" x 1 1/2". $75-$95.

Sterling silver brooch with a key piercing the heart. Marked "Sterling M. [or H] S. B., Cartier." $175-$225.

"Corocraft" sterling silver heart and key chatelaine pin. Set with red, blue, and green cabochon glass stones and rhinestones. Circa 1940, $325-$375.

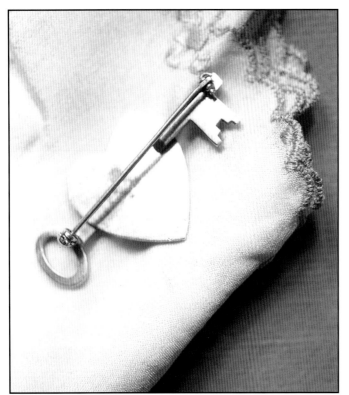

Reverse of brooch with key.

Heart-shaped chatelaine holder and three hollow keys which encase a pencil, a dip pen, and a pen knife. Marked Johann Faber, circa 1910. This piece is interesting because it is a visual pun: chatelaines originally were used to hold keys. These keys couldn't open any doors in the conventional manner, but the words that were written with them could open someone's heart! $450-$600.

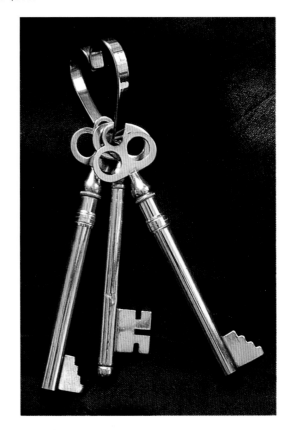

Two pencils in the shape of keys. Top: gold key with engine-turned design. $550-$625. Bottom: sterling silver key shaped like a Bramah key, made by S. Mordan & Co., circa 1880. Sampson Mordan apprenticed with Joseph Bramah at the end of the eighteenth century. Bramah invented a lock that required an unusual type of key (this lock was noted for the fact that no one was able to pick it for over half a century) as well as a quill holder. This unusual key/pencil can be seen as a way the Sampson Mordan & Company paid homage to its founder's teacher. $775-$950.

Fish pendant with jointed sections (articulated). Tag marks it as a "Napier Original." Circa 1960. A collector may enjoy the challenge of trying to find jewelry or related items with original tags, packaging, etc. $75-$95.

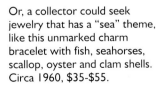

Key with faux rubies and pearls. Made by Trifari, circa 1950. $125-$225.

Or, a collector could seek jewelry that has a "sea" theme, like this unmarked charm bracelet with fish, seahorses, scallop, oyster and clam shells. Circa 1960, $35-$55.

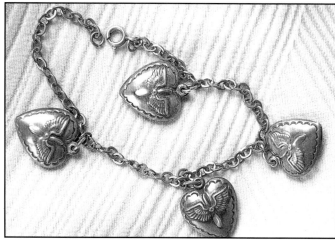

Delicate sterling silver charm bracelet consisting of four heart shaped charms with the insignia of the U. S. Air Force, circa 1942. Unsigned, $50-$75.

Sterling silver charms: 1950s stylized poodle head (we call this one "Poodle Elvis") made by "Beau," iridium plated African woman with rings on her neck and movable earrings, sterling and enamel football (1931), sterling "Danecraft" tea cup and saucer, light blue enamel on sterling silver "Beau" New York State, "R. H." sterling silver charm with enamel inlay (Panama), WWI helmet with movable chin strap, sterling and enamel Egyptian pharaoh head, sterling silver padlock signed "W.J.S.," sterling silver bell with movable clapper, sterling ice tongs with block of lucite "ice," sterling silver with black enamel officer's cap (with a tiny photo of a dog inside), sterling shoe heel with motto "No time for a Heel," sterling silver binoculars, marked with a French punch profile of an ancient Egyptian, sterling silver and enamel cross, sterling silver and cloisonné enamel teddy bear, rolled gold knitting basket with pearls and a knitting needle with a garnet tip, sterling heart, anchor and cross (faith, hope and charity). These charms were made from about 1910 to 1985, and range in value from $10-$75.

Sterling silver charm bracelet with fluted silver, carnelian, coral pate de verre and green chrysoprase beads. Circa 1950. $125-$150.

"Coro" charm bracelet with a gambling theme. Circa 1940, $225-$275.

Back to charm bracelets with original packaging, this one was made in the 1950s. Charm bracelet with chunks of bakelite, on original card. "Elvis Presley Enterprises, 1956, all rights reserved." There is a line drawing of Elvis as well as a stylized guitar on the card. $55-$75.

Sterling silver charm bracelet, circa 1960. $125-$175.

"Coro" good luck bracelet, with a lucky 7, a horseshoe, wishbone, and a real four leaf clover. $225-$275.

"Ben Casey" charm bracelet with symbols for man, woman, infinity, etc. On original card "A Bing Crosby Production Exclusive, 1962." $55-$75.

Coro charm bracelet, gold plated with turquoise. $175-$200.

"Napier" charm bracelet. Circa 1950. $350-$375.

Charm bracelet with old and new sterling silver charms: light house, cat, spiral, shell, Gloucester fisherman, heart, hammer, soccer ball, guitar, anchor, "Magic Kingdom' Disney, Cape Cod, lobster pot, baby carriage with movable wheels, wrench, working pliers, heart, cat, tools, working handcuffs, cod, baby shoe, Mayflower, etc. $350-$375.

Nineteenth century watch chain (each link is hallmarked), with a range of charms spanning the era 1860-1985: medallion watch fob (circa 1860), jade cross (circa 1960), brass Billiken (circa 1940), ivory character (circa 1870), "Tums Up" or "Touch Wood" figure in sterling silver and wood, with faceted red stones for the eyes (the hands are movable and can be raised to give two "thumbs up!" Registration mark 636612, circa 1914. This symbol was used in support of the troops during World War I.), 800 silver and gold plate with plique a jour enamel bee (from Florence, Italy, circa 1985), Japanese bronze cylindrical bead with frog and lily pad (circa 1870), sterling silver and gold owl magic pencil (circa 1870), ivory figure (circa 1860), hallmarked gold lizard (circa 1970), sterling silver bust of Nefertiti (circa 1950), white metal and cold enamel little blue man (circa 1950), sterling silver lion (circa 1960, modeled after the lions at the steps of the NYC 42nd Street public library). N.P.

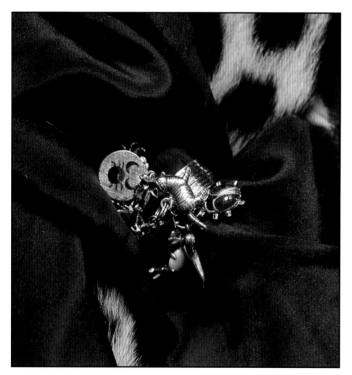

Ring with charms. 14 kt. gold, with enameled charms, some set with precious stones. Circa 1960, $990-$1,125.

Copper brooch shaped like a guitar, with multicolored glass stones, circa 1950. Finding the Elvis bracelet may remind one of an earlier passion, playing guitar, for example. $15-$25.

Copper pendant/brooch (2 1/2"), with hands playing a piano, on a chain (16"), unmarked. Or it may remind a collector of learning how to play the piano before taking up the guitar. Circa 1950. $45-$55.

"Sew on Jewels. Adds sparkle and beauty to clothes and accessories." Card with pink cut glass stones, circa 1940, $10-$15.

"Bob pin hair ornament." Bobby pins with red plastic majorettes hats on original card, circa 1950. The original card helps a collector understand fashions and advertising that were current when the object was made. $10-$15.

Rhinestone brooch in the form of a bowling ball and pin. Circa 1950. Hobbies and interests that were part of one's youth can be the subject for a collection. $25-$35.

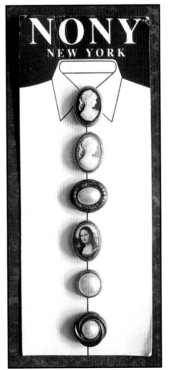

Button covers on original cardboard, circa 1960. The Mona Lisa could decorate your blouse!

Glass and metal necklace, hand-crafted, unmarked. 22", circa 1960. Reading *Sea Glass* by Anita Shreve when I saw this necklace, I couldn't resist it. It reminded me of the bits of sea glass that were collected by the main character in the book. $35-$40.

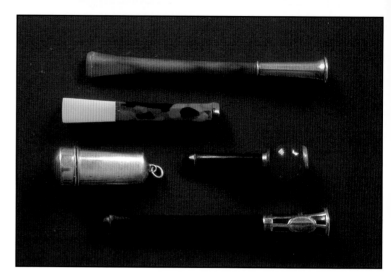

Bakelite and silver cigarette holders, circa 1930. Another subject to collect would be objects that are no longer in use, or in an area that is rapidly becoming obsolete. $55-$150. *Courtesy of Rachel Durland.*

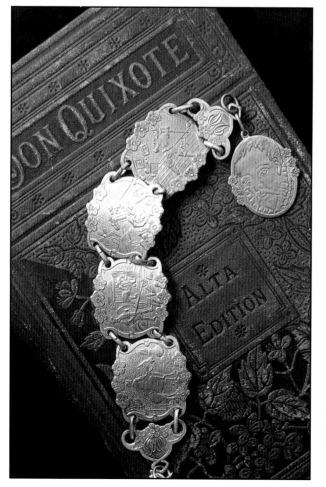

String of natural coral, circa 1950. Styles come in and out of vogue. A few years ago, no one would have worn this necklace. Now, similar ones are very popular. $75-$125.

This bracelet was inspired (as was I!) by *Don Quixote* by Cervantes. Circa 1950, silver wash over brass, with scenes from the book and a portrait of Cervantes. $25-$35.

A Special Find

*F*ebruary 2002, Philadelphia: Brooch (1 1/2" x 1 1/2"), die-stamped mixed metals (silver and brass), art nouveau, circa 1890. Unmarked. Heavy-lidded woman in a pond, with flowing hair and a wreath of flowers on her head. She looks slightly downward, to the left, and appears to be unaware of any other presence. Her right shoulder is visible, but her other shoulder is covered by her hair, which flows into and becomes indistinguishable from the ripples in the water. Lily pads and water lilies float around and in front of her, with one lily pad partially draped over her right shoulder. The image was created as a vignette, suggesting that it's a part of a larger scene, cropped to conform with the art nouveau style. The image is accentuated by both the black of the oxidation and the deliberate exposure of the brass through the silver.

Silver plated (or mixed metal) brooch, circa 1880. $175-$225.

Sometimes you have to follow your intuition. When I first saw this piece, I was captivated by how lovely it was. It couldn't be a more perfect representation of art nouveau; the beautiful young woman with flowing hair, rippling water, flowers, and the whiplash curves capture the fluidity of movement so essential to the style. What held me back was that the brooch is not solid sterling silver. By and large, plated items are less valuable than those that are made of solid metal.

However, this piece intrigued me because of the composition, the expression on the young woman's face as she appears to be looking slightly over her shoulder. She looks like a real, identifiable person, not a stylized character.

I found the portrait of the young woman engaging; she reminded me of my beautiful daughters. Despite the fact that the pin is not made of silver, I decided to purchase it. Because the brooch was reasonably priced, buying it was not a big risk. I considered having it replated, until I examined it more carefully and discovered how selectively the brass under-metal was exposed. It's visible not just in areas where the silver would have been worn through, but also in lower areas. The gold color was definitely meant to enhance the beauty of the piece as much as the oxidation was. Without the varied tones in the face, from the white silver, range of grays, and the gold color of the brass, it would not be as realistic. Replating or over-polishing would destroy this effect. It is fortunate that it still has its original patina, that no one sought to improve it by overzealously cleaning it. Examining this piece has taught me that there are beautiful examples of jewelry that I would have passed over if I could find (and afford to purchase) exclusively sterling silver or gold. It has also made me realize that learning more about the era in which the jewelry was created has allowed me to become aware of what was done originally and on purpose, so that I can recognize a good example when I see it.

Another wonderful example of silver-plated Victorian jewelry is a choker comprised of fifteen segments, linked together so that the piece maintains some flexibility without falling into the draped curve typical of most necklaces. A variety of appliqué forms adorn the choker: owls, a dog's head, personified half moons, frogs, shells, clusters of berries, bats, and a turtle. It's whimsical and definitely evokes smiles! This piece does not have the intrinsic value of a similar one made of sterling silver, nor does it have the status of being signed by a major maker (Shiebler, for example). But it is a great necklace.

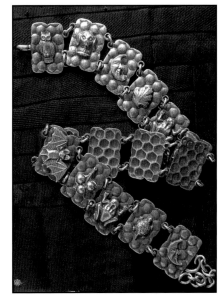

Dog collar or choker. This necklace is made of plated silver and each segment has an appliquéd image of a dog, bat, smiling crescent moon, owl, frog, etc. $225-$350.

Original Finishes

*W*e are accustomed to silver jewelry being a uniformly shiny blue-white gray. While we see oxidized silver fairly regularly, we rarely see silver that has been finished in a "dead white" and we do not often see silver mixed with other metals. Yet, these finishes and styles were popular in the mid- to late 1800s, and were purposely created to enhance the variety of colors in silver. In a book published in 1866, the following cleaning and polishing compound is recommended: "Aqua ammonia 1 oz.; prepared chalk 1/2 oz; mix, and keep corked. To use, for rings and other smooth-surfaced jewelry, wet a bit of cloth with the compound after having shaken it, and rub the article thoroughly; then polish by rubbing with a silk handkerchief or piece of soft buckskin. For articles which are rough surfaced, use a suitable brush." (Chase, p. 250.) These instructions describe how to polish both smooth and rough surfaced metal, acknowledging that not all silver was meant to be shiny and uniform in its finish.

A formula for "frosting and whitening silver" was provided by B. Frank Van Cleve in 1874: "Sulphuric acid, 1 dr.; water, 4 oz.; heat the pickle, and immerse the silver in until frosted as desired; then wash off clean, and dry with a soft linen cloth, or in a fine clean saw-dust. For whitening only, a smaller portion of acid may be used." (Van Cleve, pp. 245-246.) Or, a "bright gold tinge may be given to silver by steeping it for a suitable length of time in a weak solution of sulphuric acid and water strongly impregnated with iron-rust." (Van Cleve, p. 246.) A formula for frosting polished silver was provided by R. Moore in 1881: "cyanide of potassium 1 oz.; dissolved in 1/2 pt. of water. Do not hold the silver in your hands, but use pliers made of lance wood or box wood, and apply the mixture with a brush to the polished surface." In this process, the copper alloy is eaten away by the acid, and the pure silver remains. "The beauty of fine silver is given to the surface by boiling the silver in a copper vessel containing very dilute sulphuric acid which dissolves out the copper of the alloy and leaves the silver dead white; it is then burnished and exhibits its proper beauty of color and luster. (Silliman, p. 8.)

Moore also described how to create designs of gold on silver, or of silver on gold: "select a smooth part of the silver, and sketch on it a monogram or any design you choose, with a sharp lead pencil, then place the article in a gold solution with the battery in good working order, and in a short time all the parts not sketched with the lead pencil will be covered with the coat of gold. After cleansing the article, the black lead is easily removed by the fingers, and the silver ornament is disclosed. A gold ornament may be produced by reversing the process." (Moore, p. 341.)

In 1894, Martin Brunor praised the use of a sandblaster for obtaining a satin finish. He explains that because many small items would be ruined by acid, "with the sandblasting apparatus … there is no risk of spoiling the goods or enlarging the holes; as fine a matt as desired may be obtained." (Brunor, p. 67.)

Gold was made in a variety of colors and finished both as a shiny surface and as a somewhat matt finish, usually called a Roman finish. Color could range from "extra red" to "pale red," white, yellow, "pale yellow," green, "greenish," and "yellowish-grey," as gold could be alloyed with copper and silver, cadmium, iron or steel. (Gee, pp. 181-261) Gold could also vary in its purity, and could be anywhere from 9 carat up. For example, a formula for 9-carat gold alloy for "collar studs in one piece of metal" would include fine gold, fine silver, pure copper, and compo No. 4.

Mixed Metals

The Japanese excelled at mixed metal work, and American designers did their best to emulate this extraordinary style. Mixed metal pieces are like tiny paintings, however, metal is used in place of paint.

Any of these finishes can be destroyed by polishing. If you are lucky enough to find a piece with its original patina, resist the temptation to polish it and learn to love it the way it is.

Planting Diamonds

*A*s you begin to learn more about jewelry, you will find information coming from unexpected sources. Although I was amused while reading that eighteenth century aristocrats fabricated the story that diamonds reproduced themselves and gave birth to baby diamonds in order to explain the increasing number of stones that they wore (read Kunz, *The Curious Lore Of Gems*), I never expected that I would hear an equally interesting (but true) story from someone I knew.

One day one of my daughters and I were visiting an old friend. We sat outside, enjoying his beautiful garden, as we talked about our various projects. I mentioned that I was working on another book, one on jewelry, and our friend Em told us this remarkable story.

In 1924, Emmanuel Kuna was the six year old son of an emigrant Bohemian artisan. His father, employed by William Scheer, designed and fabricated the prototypes for jewelry that was retailed by renowned firms Cartier and Van Cleef and Arpels. The jewelry he designed was often created for a particular client, and for this reason Kuna would carefully paint the wax model to emulate the metal in which the piece would ultimately be cast. He would set actual stones, usually diamonds and sapphires, into the wax prototype ring or brooch, so the customer could try the piece on to determine her satisfaction with the style, its proportions, and the number and size of the gems; all this before the piece was actually cast.

The economy was booming and there were more than enough eager customers to keep the Scheer business active. When Em and his sister greeted his father at the train in Glen Rock, New Jersey, when he came home from his workday in New York City, he would always be carrying a briefcase filled with "jobs" to be completed at home that evening. After dinner he would resume painting the wax models and select actual stones to be set from an array he brought home each evening.

Em was fascinated with the glittery gems, and often watched his father work. An inquisitive young man, he asked his father where the gems came from. His father, perhaps trying to give a short answer to a complex question, answered simply that the stones grew in the earth. He continued his work while Em began to plot, imagining himself picking a crop of diamonds. Em was already quite fond of gardening, and decided that if he were to plant some diamonds, fertilize and water them like any other plant, they would grow and might even multiply.

One day, not too many days after Em had asked his father where diamonds came from, his father surprised his family by coming home early from work. When Em and his sister saw him walking towards the house mid-afternoon, they ran to him expecting smiles and some sort of holiday. But Mr. Kuna was somber. He entered the house, set his briefcase on the kitchen table, and told his wife to summon each one of the children. Em knew something was wrong, but didn't know what. Soon all the children sat soundlessly around the kitchen table as Mr. Kuna spoke. He told his family that when he had arrived at the office earlier in the day and had opened his briefcase, he found that all the packets of loose gems were empty. He told his family that the night before his briefcase contained many very expensive gems. He asked his children, very deliberately, if any of them had taken anything from the case the night before.

Em, after a pause, spoke. "Yes, Father," he said. "I took the gems and planted them so they would grow." His father stood up, took Em by the hand, and asked where he had planted them. Together, they went out to the back yard, where Em showed his father the neat row where he had carefully tapped the diamonds out of the packets, covered them with soil and watered them as if they were seeds.

Mr. Kuna and Em dug and found each and every diamond that Em had so lovingly planted. Em told us "I knew exactly where they were. I was quite meticulous. I had cleaned a space by the back porch, removing the leaves from the ground just as I had seen my father do. I dug a trench and spaced the stones, emeralds and diamonds—not chips but real stones—carefully covering them over, patting the soil. But they weren't in the ground long enough to sprout!" Unfortunately for Em, though, his father was from the old school and Em says that he remembers the spanking he got till this day.

The wax models and artwork shown in this section were made by Em's father. The Depression hit the jewelry industry hard, and Mr. Kuna lost his job with Scheer. He spent the rest of his life as a landscaper, and through his influence Em continued to learn how to make things grow. He was especially good at growing friendships. Em did not live to see this book published, but we are sure he is up there still nurturing those he loved.

Mr. Kuna created jewelry in the 1920s Art Deco style. We are fortunate to have all these wonderful examples to show the reader how the pieces were designed. Some of the styles are identical to actual jewelry marked "Cartier," particularly the Greek temples.

Jewelry that followed is often labeled "Retro." It is modernistic and elegant, and the examples shown from a 1930s catalog exhibit traits in common with the jewelry designed by Kuna.

Em Kuna's parents,
circa 1940.

Kuna at four years old, circa 1919. At
about the age when he planted the gems.

Em Kuna in his garden,
2002.

Wax model of brooch
designed by Kuna.

Watercolor of sapphire and
diamond brooch designed by Kuna.

Partially painted model of brooch designed by Kuna.

Painted model of pavé diamond floral brooch.

Painted model of a pavé diamond brooch in the shape of a terrier.

Painted model of a pavé diamond and sapphire brooch in the shape of a whippet.

ABOUT 225-235 DIA'S AND 26 SAPF'S.

Wax model of a setter.

Wax model of a greyhound.

Wax model of a running horse.

Wax model of a flying duck.

Wax model of a flying duck.

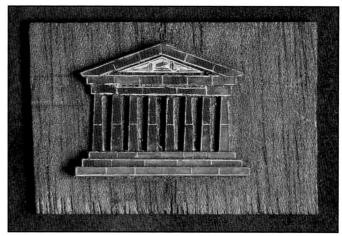

Wax model of a Greek temple.

Wax model of a Greek temple.

Another temple.

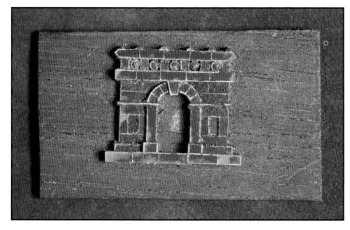

Wax model of a Greek temple.

Partially painted wax
model for a ring.

Partially painted wax
model for a ring.

Model of a ring.

Wax model of a ring made by Em Kuna,
Senior. Circa 1920, this model captures the
effect of marquis-cut diamonds radiating
from a large central diamond.

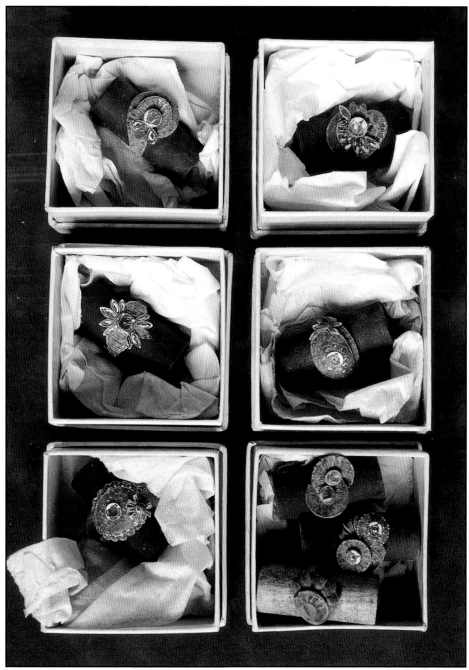

Models of rings in original boxes.

Two diamond rings

Filigree and daimond ring. NP.

Modern Creations in Gold and Platinum, circa 1940.
8 1/2" x 11", 48 pages. $35-$50.

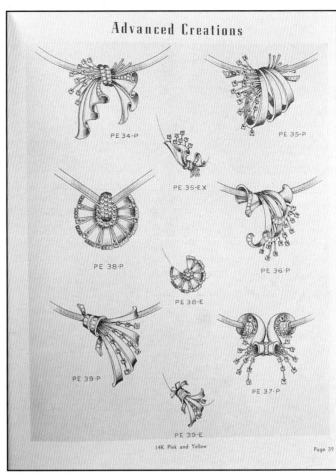

Illustration of "Advanced Designs" retro pendants and brooches.

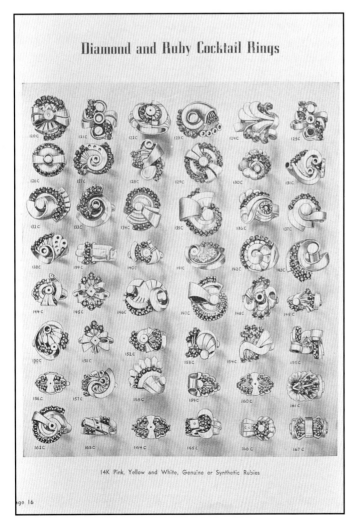

Page showing examples of "Diamond and Ruby Cocktail Rings."

Retro style brooch, rose and yellow gold plated with marquis cut pink stones. Approximately 2", unmarked. Circa 1935. $50-$75.

Retro brooch with blue cut glass sapphires. 3", $75-$150. *Courtesy of Ruth Taylor.*

Retro brooch/pendant, vermeil. Set with cut glass diamonds and rubies. Unmarked, 2" x 1 3/4", $75-$125.

Retro brooch with teardrop-shaped faux emeralds, 4", $75-$150. *Courtesy of Ruth Taylor.*

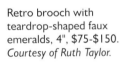

Retro brooch, marked "1/20 12 k. g. f. I. H". With rose and yellow gold plating and molded green glass stones. 2 1/2" x 2", $45-$65.

Retro brooch. *Courtesy of Ruth Taylor.*

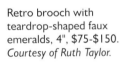

Retro brooch, stylized flower and ribbons. 2", marked "14 k. g. f." $75-$100.

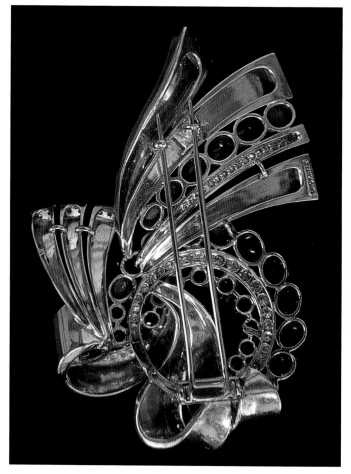

Retro brooch, signed "Lackritz." Cabochon rubies, channel set diamonds, 14 kt. gold, 2" x 3", double pin back. $7,500-$8,500. *Courtesy of Ruth Taylor.*

Reverse of previous brooch.

Retro style bracelet. Calibré diamonds, cabochon rubies, 14 kt. gold. $6,500-$7,500. *Courtesy of Ruth Taylor.*

Sterling silver with a gold wash retro style brooch. Marked "sterling," 3" x 1 1/2". $75-$125.

This dynamic brooch is marked "Sterling" and is 4" long and 1" wide. The wing shapes are plated with a rose colored gold, and the square-cut pink glass stones are set in a white metal. $35-$55.

Vermeil retro brooch. Circa 1940, Signed Coro. $250-$325.

Marked "Sterling" brooch in the shape of a ballerina. 3 1/2" x 2", gold-washed, with open-backed prong-set red, white, and blue faceted glass stones. $150-$175.

This 3 1/2" x 2" brooch appears to be hand-fabricated, with the drill and saw marks still evident. The center of the stone seems to be a lighter shade of green because light shows through where the back is pierced. $75-$125.

Fur clip (with two long prongs attached to the top and two smaller ones attached to the bottom on the back), vermeil, with clear rhinestones and faceted amber colored glass stone. 2 1/2" x 1", $65-$75.

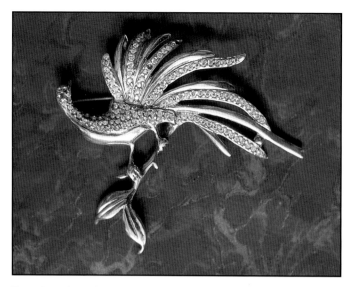

Brooch marked "Sterling" in the shape of a bird on a branch, displaying his rhinestone plumage. 2 1/2" x 2 1/2", $75-$100.

Art Deco ring with diamonds and emerald. *Courtesy of Anna Reiss.* N.P.

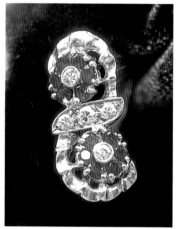

Ring, gold with diamonds and rubies. Retro modern, $650-$750. *Courtesy of Ruth Taylor.*

Art Deco necklace, 1930-1940. This necklace is a bold example of the costume jeweler's art. It consists of a snake chain centered between beaded metal chains that flow into three tubes on each side of the large (2") mirror-backed faceted glass stone (the light hits the glass in a manner similar to the way light reflects off a disco ball) $150-$225.

Retro modern ring with diamonds and rubies in a buckle design. $2,500-$3,200. *Courtesy of Ruth Taylor.*

Filigree bracelet with diamonds and saphires. *Courtesy of Tom and Mary Valentino of Others' Oldies.* $5000-$6000.

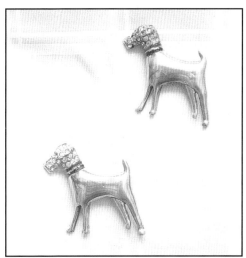

Dogs in silver. $150-$175 pair.

Gold and rose cut diamond brooch in a crescent shape. $2,800-$3,000. *Courtesy Adele Golden of The Garden Gate Antiques, Philadelphia.*

Art Deco filigree (white gold) bracelet with diamonds and sapphires. $2,500-$3,500. *Courtesy of Ruth Taylor.*

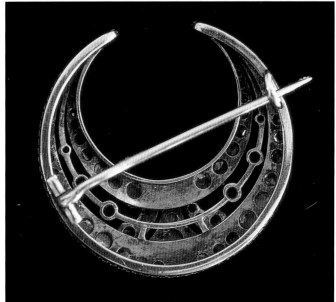

Reverse of diamond brooch.

Edwardian bar pin, silver and pastes. Marked "Fishon," $75-$125.

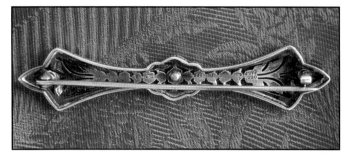

Reverse of Edwardian bar pin.

Brooch. *Courtesy of Gerald Schultz of The Antique Gallery.* $265-$285.

Reverse.

Brooch. *Courtesy of Gerald Schultz of The Antique Gallery.* $195-$225.

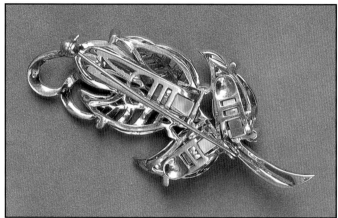

Reverse.

Marcasite necklace, circa 1910. Silver, carnelian, and marcasite, $150-$175.

Marcasite and moonstone brooch, marked "Sterling, Germany" circa 1950, 1 3/4" x 1", $125-$150.

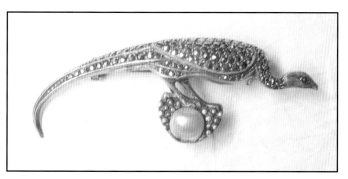

935 silver and marcasite brooch, signed with a Theodore Fahrner logo. Peacock with a red cabochon stone eye, perched on a blister pearl orb, 2 1/4"x 3/4". Circa 1920. $425-$500.

Silver and marcasite bracelets. N.P. *Private collection.*

Silver and marcasite bracelets. N.P. *Private collection.*

Silver and marcasite bracelets. N.P. *Private collection.*

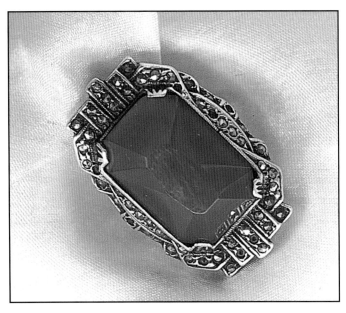

Sterling silver and marcasite ring, circa 1920. *Private collection.* NP (no price).

Sterling silver and marcasite clips, circa 1920. *Private collection.* NP (no price).

Reverse.

Three dress clips, c. 1930. $50-$75.

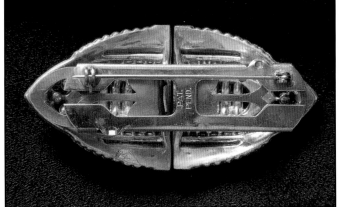

Reverse.

14 kt gold ring, onyx stone with a diamond chip set in the center of a gold four-leaf clover, circa 1930. $350-$400. *Courtesy Tom and Mary Valentino of Other's Oldies.*

Right and below:
Garnet ring. $250-$325.

Art Deco ring: platinum with rubies and diamonds (1.20 carats plus 55 point center stone). $3,150-$3,350. *Courtesy Tom and Mary Valentino of Other's Oldies.*

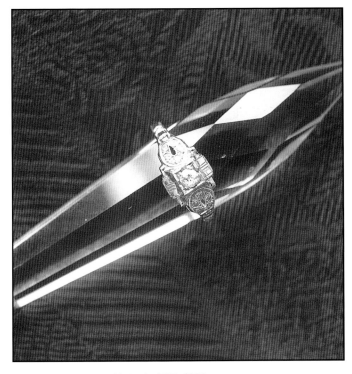

Diamond ring, new old stock. $250-$325.

Art Nouveau ring, gold, onyx, diamond. Circa 1900, $225-$275.

Two gold and turquoise rings, circa 1890. Turquoise rings may range in value from $50-$350.

Amethyst, pearl, and gold ring, circa 1900.

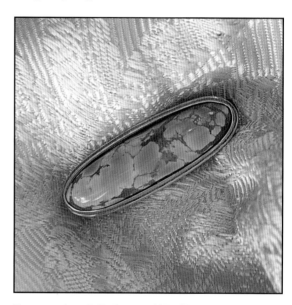

Turquoise Arts & Crafts ring. $275-$300.

Turquoise brooches. *Courtesy of Adele Golden of Garden Gates Antiques.* $250-$350.

Silver and turquoise ring.

Turquoise and silver rings. Turquoise rings may range in value from $50-$350.

"Azure Turquoises Do Not Change Color" ad from *The Century Illustrated Magazine*, December 1899, page 54 of the advertising section. In this ad, the Azure Turquoise Company proclaims that while turquoise is one of the most popular stones of the moment, people are fearful of purchasing stones that may turn color. Azure Turquoise was marked and guaranteed not to change.

Sterling silver brooch with cabochon turquoise, "Firenza" in script. From a tour of Italy at the end of the nineteenth century. $75-$125.

Turquoise necklace and bracelet, circa 1950. $50-$75.

Velvet choker with hand sewn turquoise beads and fringe. Circa 1885, $75-$125.

Oval ivory beads, necklace, circa 1930. $125-$150.

Portrait of a young woman wearing a similar choker, not signed, but dated 1884.

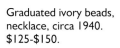

Graduated turquoise beads. Necklace, circa 1950. $75-$125.

Faux coral beads, necklace, circa 1940. $50-$75.

Graduated ivory beads, necklace, circa 1940. $125-$150.

Lava (limestone) earrings, with gold bezels and kidney wire. Man and woman face each other. Circa 1880, $275-$325.

Serendipitous Moments

*T*oday, for example, after enjoying a lovely lunch in town with my good friend Rachel Marks (antiques dealer *par excellence*, owner of "Rachel Marks Antiques." You will see her name repeatedly in the captions in this book, under some of the most beautiful silver jewelry ever made), we walked over to "Desires," an aptly-named jewelry store. The owner, Scott Mikolay, had shown me some designs that his grandfather had drawn for jewelry he produced in the late 1930s and 1940s (which he kindly allowed me to photograph). As we were trying to decide which of the amazing necklaces we would buy if we won a million dollars, Bill and Hillary walked by. I don't think they would have to wait to win the lottery before they could buy anything they wanted, but who knows? It was good to see that they were supporting local businesses.

Another serendipitous moment occurred when I was at the "Masterpieces of American Jewelry" exhibit (Museum of Folk Art, fall 2004). A very nice person commented on how much he liked the brooch I was wearing. Before long he introduced himself as Larry Vrba. Larry designed for Miriam Haskell and creates his own spectacular jewelry today. I will take up his invitation to interview him for the next book!

Another day I was doing my homework at one of the high, high end retail stores in a local mall. This research involved drooling over very expensive costume jewelry while examining it and talking to the saleswomen about what made it so special. One of the saleswomen, it turned out, used to work for Kenneth Jay Lane. Marcia Coltin very kindly introduced me to Mr. Lane, which was one of the highlights of my research.

"Har" fortune teller, circa 1950. We can't predict the serendipitous moments that lead us to greater understanding. $325-$375.

Inspiration

*J*ewelry designers are inspired by a variety of sources. Perhaps the most traditional, most universal springboard for design is nature. Creating jewelry in the form of flowers, foliage, insects, animals, craftsmen have long attempted to satisfy the urge to make the ephemeral eternal. Natural flowers may wilt and turn brown, a bouquet made of gold will be everlasting. Jewelry reflects the styles and symbolism of each era, and certain forms and meanings are more popular during one age than another.

For example, images of snakes weave in and out of vogue, and when they are in, they may be symbols of sensuality or symbolic of everlasting love. Nature may be represented as clear and accessible, symmetrical and reasoned, or seductively enigmatic. The manner in which the jeweler of one age depicts objects from nature reflects the way life was perceived then and that attitude (or those attitudes) would be evident in current philosophy, literature, music, and painting. Jewelry styles would align with popular culture.

In class societies, the upper classes would set a pace that was met more and more rapidly as industrialization, allowed those of the less privileged classes to purchase jewelry that was less expensive, true, but the jewelry they were now able to buy closely resembled the styles that they sought to emulate. That, in turn, fueled the process as the wealthy upped the bar, causing more change and a greater emphasis on novelty. It's fascinating to study the decorative arts of the Victorian era and to observe how jewelry styles changed at a progressively faster velocity, how the pace quickened with time. The brief Edwardian period spawned styles that, while still Victorian in some senses, led to a modern period that belies our perception of an era where women were still wearing long skirts and when horses were more common a mode of transportation than automobiles.

Another source of ideas for designs is history. During the nineteenth century, there were revivals of all sorts: Gothic Revival, Egyptian Revival, Neoclassical Revival, etc. The magnificent exhibit of Castellani jewelry at the Bard Graduate Center in New York underscored the outstanding workmanship that made this archeological revival extraordinary.

This historical approach to collecting is based on finding jewelry made in a style inspired by an earlier culture. The Egyptian influence, for example, is seen repeatedly, with variations that reflect current trends. Egyptian art is colorful, mysterious, and intriguing, lending itself to adaptation. Some Art Deco jewelry has an Egyptian influence, but so does jewelry that was created in the 1870s. There are at least two Egyptian Revival periods in the time frame that this book covers. The first began in the early 1870s, with the opening of the Suez Canal and Verdi's opera *Aida*. The event which prompted the second was the discovery and opening of Tutanhaken's tomb by Howard Carter in 1922. When the treasures of King Tut's tomb were exhibited in the United States in the 1970s, Egyptomania struck once more, as it will again whenever the impressive exhibit returns (at the time of this writing, another exhibition was pending, this time accompanied by reconstructions of what the young Tut may have looked like).

Millennia before the term costume jewelry was employed, Egyptians mixed precious with non-precious and thought the color and form of the jewelry more important than the intrinsic value of the metals and stones. Glass, faience, and paste beads were mixed with carnelian and gold beads. The Egyptians may have sought immortality by mummifying human remains, but it is perhaps through its immensely appealing jewelry that Egyptians have truly become immortal.

Reading books that were written during the era you are interested in is also an excellent way to learn more about jewelry. *In The Land of the Almighty Dollar*, Gordon asked fellow Brits to send best wishes for the upcoming year of 1892. He quotes Charles Dickens as saying, "Your American learned woman remains a woman in spite of her learning. She dresses well, and tries to look as well as she can—not to please the men; oh no! but to please herself." (Gordon, p. 82.)

According to an article in *The Cosmopolitan*, "Never before in any era have jewels been so universally and profusely worn as at the present day. A particular fad of the hour is the wearing of gems en suite. One woman of great social distinction has appeared lately wearing a quantity of sapphires unrelieved by even the white contrasting luster of an occasional diamond. Another has worn only opals—rings, necklace, brooches, etc., unaccompanied by any other stone … There is no sign of any lessening of the number of rings with which women cover their fingers. Indeed, more have been crowded on, to such an extent that it was hinted in Paris last spring that gloves were to be discarded because of the difficulty in getting them over gem incrusted fingers … Another apparently ephemeral fad to which women have persistently clung is the adoption of long, swinging chains of gold and ropes of jewels or beads …" (*The Cosmopolitan*, November 1903, pp. 16-17.) This description of an "Oriental bangle" may cause the reader to smile. The bracelet "from which every imaginable article in miniature as once with charms for the chatelaine may be suspended. Kettles, masks, opera-glasses, teapots, cups, goblets, skulls with ruby or diamond eyes, mice, dolls, Harlequins, cupids, clowns" (*Demorest's Magazine*, January 1878). This was the era that Phrenology was considered a legitimate study, one that would enable one to understand the workings of a person's mind through measuring the size of each 'cerebral organ.' …" Dr. Gall was at last led to conclude, first, that the brain is an aggregate of many different parts, each serving for the manifestation of a particular mental faculty; and secondly that, all other conditions being equal, the size of each of these cerebral organs is a measure of the power of its function." (De Puy, p. 1372.)

Another way to understand jewelry of the past century is to select a certain subject or object and note how it is depicted in each decade or each style. The examples that follow are an insect timeline, so to speak. En tremblant bee, circa 1870, 2" x 1 1/4". Gold brooch (can also be worn as a pendent) with rose cut diamonds in silver settings and rubies. $3,500-$4,500. *Courtesy of Ruth Taylor.*

En tremblant bee (brooch or pendant) with cabochon garnets, emerald eyes, rose cut diamonds. Circa 1880, 1 1/4" x 1 1/2", $2,000-$2,500. *Courtesy of Ruth Taylor.*

Reverse of the bee.

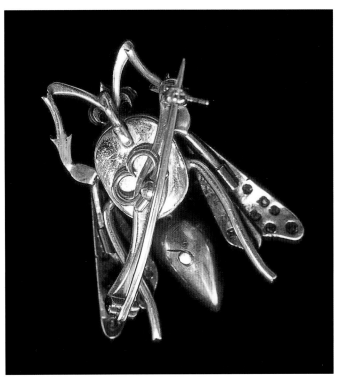

Reverse of bee.

Crenellated locket, circa 1890. Mixed metal (silver, rose gold, yellow gold) in the Japanese style, with appliquéd bird and butterfly. $250-$275.

Art Nouveau brooch made of stamped and gilded brass, with artificial pearls and Bohemian opalescent glass stone. In the shape of a fly poised between leaves. 2 1/2" x 2", circa 1910, $175-$225.

Brooch with butterfly engraved in reverse on glass cabochon, fused with gold and opalescence. Bohemia, circa 1900. 1 1/2" x 1". $65-$75.

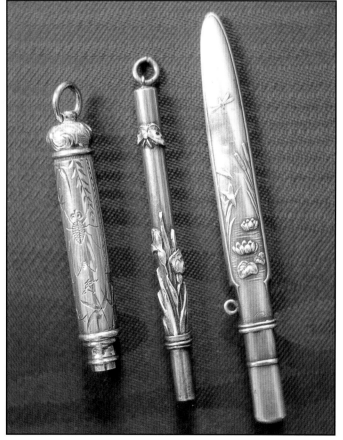

Left: Sterling silver and gold magic pencil with hand-engraved aesthetic pattern (inspired by the Japanese) including a fly. Marked "Mabie Todd & Co.," circa 1870. 2" x 1/4" closed, $475-$575. Center: Sterling silver and cloisonné enamel pencil, with a butterfly fluttering over irises. Marked with a Japanese signature. 2 1/2" long, circa 1880, $250-$350. Right: Repoussé silver vest pocket pencil with a dragonfly hovering over a pond with cat tails and water lilies. Marked "Johann Faber Paris Deposé," 3 1/4" x 1/2", $400-$550.

Dragonfly, with hand-cut glass stones and painted enamel wings, marked Czechoslovakia, circa 1915. 2 1/4" x 1 1/2", $45-$65.

Art Deco cicada. Stamped body, lapis lazuli tail, pavé set clear glass stones, glued in place (except for the prong-set antenna). Circa 1930, $45-$65.

"Castlecliff" brooch in the shape of flower with a bee landing on it. Missing some clear glass stones. Cold enamel on white metal, circa 1935. $65-$75.

Large beetle, marked "Sterling." With red, white, and blue cut glass prong-set stones. 3" x 1 1/4", circa 1945. $150-$225.

Silver flies on brooch (2" x 3") and earrings (1" x 3/4"), marked "Sterling." 1940s, $150-$225 (set).

Stylized insect, white metal (gold plated), with a very large faceted, unfoiled glass citrine, rubies, and diamantes. Circa 1935, 2 1/2" x 2", $75-$125.

Signed "Shreiner" insects, en tremblant, circa 1950. $400-$475 for the pair. *Courtesy of Ruth Taylor.*

Left: Moth trembler. Right: "Art" dragonfly. Bottom: Butterfly with green cut glass stones set into clear plastic. $75-$150. *Courtesy of Ruth Taylor.*

Left: Green prong set glass stones in blackened brass mount, marked "Weiss." Late 1940s, early 1950s, 1 1/2" x 1", $75-$95. Right: Butterfly in gold wash with faux prong-set amethyst wings. Unmarked, circa 1950, 1" x 3/4", $35-$45.

En tremblant moth, with baroque faux pearl body and pavé glass stones, signed "Pauline Rader." 2" x 1 1/2", 1950s, $150-$175.

En tremblant butterfly, pavé set clear glass cut stones and a gold wash, signed "Nettie Rosenstein." 2 1/4" x 1 1/2", pre-1955, $175-$275.

Bug, signed "Har," after 1955. Simulated gold and silver metal, ruby cut glass eyes, and pavé set clear cut glass stones on body, $75-$125.

"Miriam Haskell" comb with a butterfly, circa 1950. $75-$95.

"Rebajes" copper butterfly, circa 1950. $75-$125.

Insect brooch, signed "Art ©", circa 1960. Cabochon emerald cut glass stones, pavé set diamantes in wings and head, topaz colored cut glass eyes. $45-$75.

Trembling bug with white pâte de verre stones on body and wings, and green cut glass eyes glued in place. Unsigned, 1960s, 1 3/4" x 2". $45-$65 (the blurry wings in the photograph show the motion of the wings).

Rhinestone butterfly brooch, Kenneth Lane ("© KJL), 2 1/2" x 2 3/4". Sapphire blue, cerulean blue, aquamarine marquis glass stones, frosted brilliants, one baguette stone, all prong set. Circa 1960, $125-$150.

Butterfly pendant in the Chinese style, signed "Kenneth Lane ©." 1960s, 3 1/2" x 3", 52" double chain, $125-$175.

Butterfly, "Morpho Menelaus" from Peru. This is the kind of color jewelers were inspired to emulate (or, in the case of these earrings, actually utilize) in their jewelry. $30.

Earrings, palm trees and shoreline painted in silhouette over iridescent butterfly wings, in round settings with glass crystal, 1/2". Circa 1930, $25-$50.

The "real thing:" pansy earring made by Hedges, Newark, NJ. Late nineteenth century. Fine enamel work on 14 kt. gold, with seed pearl. Marked with Hedges logo. It is important to understand the qualities that make a piece of fine jewelry extraordinary. It is equally important to note the characteristics of well-made costume jewelry. Set, $275-$350.

Costume jewelry in the form of a bouquet of violets, unmarked. $30.

Earrings, with tropical scene painted on top of iridescent butterfly wings fitted into rectangular mounts, under glass crystal. Circa 1930, $25-$50.

Reverse view comparing the backs of the two previous pieces. Focus on "Hedges" logo, top left.

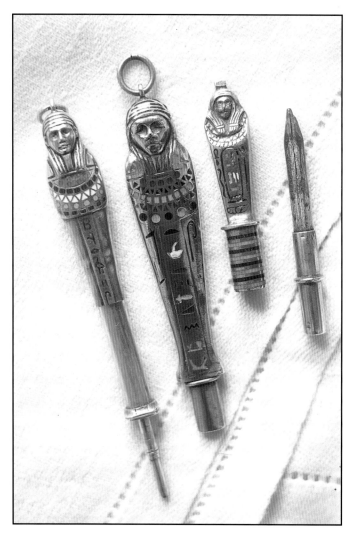

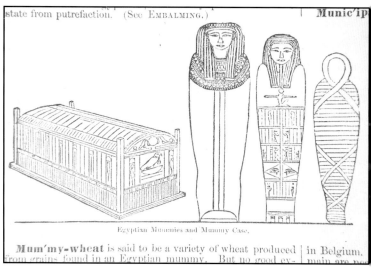

Mummies and mummy case, from *People's Cyclopedia*, Volume II, page 1202.

Pencils: early magic pencil in the shape of a mummy, finely articulated. Gold, silver, blue, white, red, turquoise, and green enamel, 1 1/2" closed, 3" open. No maker's mark. Circa 1875, $350-$425. Unusual flat or vest pocket pencil in 800 silver, with red, green, turquoise, blue, and white enamel work. 2 1/2", circa 1880. $325-$400. Silver mummy case with round wooden pencil, silver ferrule. Silver with red, blue, turquoise, and white enamel, bands of enamel around plinth, circa 1880, 2". $275-$350.

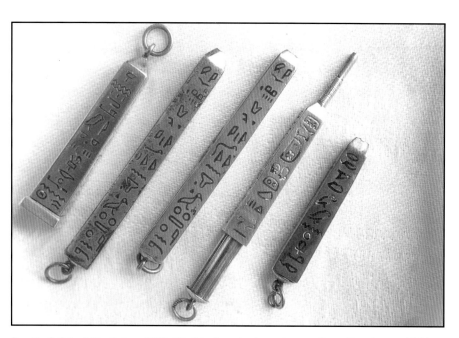

Pencils: (*left to right*, all circa 1880) Obelisk-shaped telescoping pencil, sterling silver, gold, blue enamel, 1 3/4" closed, 3" open. The removable pencil is encased within the obelisk. When the bottom is pulled, a telescoping pencil comes out, allowing the owner to write with the pencil while the obelisk remains on its chain. $350-$425. Obelisk shaped magic pencil, gold-washed metal, gold-filled trim, blue enamel, 2 1/4" closed, 3 3/4" open.

Obelisk, translation of "Cleopatra's Needle," 1884, from *People's Cyclopedia*, Volume II, page 1264.

Egyptian Influence

Pencil and fountain pen in the Egyptian style. Magic pencils shaped like mummies or pharaohs are, of all figural magic pencils, the most common. However, even these are becoming more difficult to find. Fountain pens in this form are very rare. This one is 3" long when the pen is inside the decorative silver and enamel casing, and 4 1/4" long when the silver pharaoh is posted as one would post the cap for a pen. The pen itself has a warranted gold nib, and is filled with an eyedropper. The image is highly stylized and is probably an artist's impression of what a mummy would look like. The shape of the gold pencil is far less stylized, and is a more typical rendition of a mummy. The pharaoh has his arms crossed over his chest, is holding a flail and is wearing the ceremonial beard. Pen, $750-$825. Pencil, $375-$450.

Left to right: gold Egyptian influence magic pencil (1 1/2"), silver sarcophagus (3/4") that holds the tiny gold and enamel mummy beneath it, Moses basket (3/4", silver and enamel. A tiny baby Moses would be in the basket), silver and enamel magic pencil. $75-$450.

Flat or vest pocket pencil, Egyptian influence, Art Deco. Marked "Sterling C.," circa 1930. $425-$575.

Chatelaine holder in the form of a pharaoh's head, silver, unmarked, circa 1870, 2 1/2" x 1 1/2". $225-$275.

La Magnificence des Habillements Egyptiens, title page, circa 1920.

"Ascending the pyramids, Egypt" from *Album of the World's Gems*, 1893, page 132. Tourists felt that their trip to Egypt would not be complete unless they scaled the pyramid in Giza, "… and can say that they have stood on the peak of the most gigantic human work in the world." The ability to print photographs was still relatively new in 1893, and it offered another avenue to understand the world without having to sort through verbal or written descriptions of people and places, etc. "We might well dwell upon the new history which has sprung from the investigations and witness of the eye … The leading adjunct of modern historical and scientific research is Photography … Photography may be defined as the art of making all men travelers." (Boyd, 1893, pages 3-4)

Page from *La Magnificence des Habillements Egyptiens*.

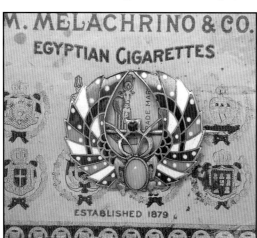

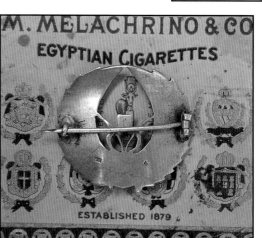

Reverse of previous brooch.

Brooch, 800 silver and enamel, with a bezel-set cabochon turquoise stone, photographed on a box of "Egyptian Cigarettes." $400-$500. *Courtesy of Giselle DeRienzo Antiques.*

Egyptian influence belt (brass), circa 1920, 26", $75-$125.

Sterling silver brooch with wings of Horus and scarab. 3" x 3/4", $65-$85. *Courtesy of Rachel Marks Antiques.*

Stylized Egyptian style brooch, with inlaid enamel and a bezel-set cabochon amethyst. Marked "F & B" (Foster and Bailey), $200-$250. *Courtesy of Giselle De Rienzo Antiques.*

Enamel brooch with stone scarab, $125-$175. *Courtesy of Giselle De Rienzo Antiques.*

Scarab with lotus flowers, brooch, with indecipherable hallmark. $175-$250. *Courtesy of Giselle De Rienzo Antiques.*

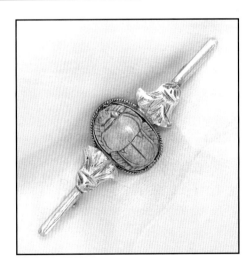

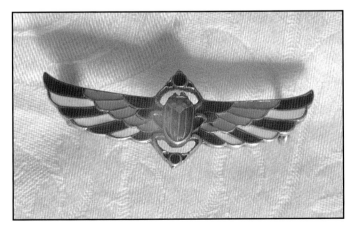

Silver and cloisonné brooch, 1 3/4" x 1/2", marked 800. $55-$75.

Brooch with the bust of a pharaoh surrounded with enameled lotus blossoms. Marked 800, with a gold wash. $250-$350. *Courtesy of Giselle De Rienzo Antiques.*

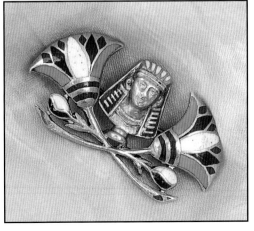

Brooch and key ring in the Egyptian style. $175-$250. *Courtesy of Giselle De Rienzo Antiques.*

Color photograph illustrating Egyptian motifs in enameled jewelry (page 132 from Daniel Low catalogue, *Yearbook for 1910*). The Egyptian style was adapted to jewelry in a remarkable array of styles: the Revivalist, Art Nouveau, Art Deco, mid- to late twentieth century costume jewelry, etc. Perhaps immortality was attained after all, through the appeal of imagery that originated millennia ago.

Reverse of brooch and key ring.

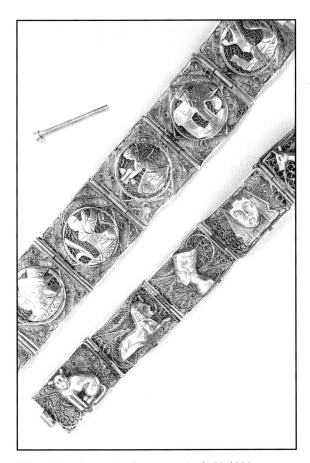

Filigree bracelets in the Egyptian style. $150-$250.
Courtesy of Giselle De Rienzo Antiques.

Pendant with red glass cameo in the Egyptian style, with a finish that gives it the appearance of being an archeological find. Chain 22", pendant with drop 2 1/2" x 1". Circa 1925, $125-$150.

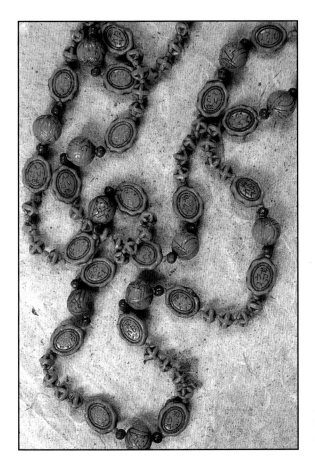

Yellow pâte de verre beads with scarabs and seated pharaoh. Circa 1920. $75-$125. *Courtesy of Giselle De Rienzo Antiques*.

Green and brown glass beads made in Bohemia, in the Egyptian style, impressed with imitation hieroglyphics. Each bead hand-knotted, 38", circa 1920. $75-$125.

Gold cufflinks with hand painted enamel profile portraits of pharaohs. Marked with patent number 2472953. $900-$1,200. *Courtesy of Giselle Rienzo Antiques.*

Orange, burnt sienna, deep red, and green glass bead necklace with pharaohs heads, pyramids, and hieroglyphs. Marked "Registered" (32" with 5" drop and pendants). Circa 1920, $250-$300.

Stud, gold-filled over brass, inlaid, hand-painted enamel portrait of a youthful Egyptian. Circa 1890. $75-$125.

Trade Cards

*T*rade cards were used to advertise businesses as early as the late 1700s. However, the field burgeoned after the Civil War. The process for printing in color (chromolithography) had been perfected, and now trade cards could be multi-colored. Chromolithography is an involved process, which entails a different stone for each color. Lithography is planographic, meaning that the ink is printed directly (but in reverse) from the surface of a polished limestone or other prepared plate. Each color must be registered perfectly or the image will appear unfocused. While this may not seem like a major accomplishment to us because we are so accustomed to seeing color reproductions in books and magazines, all one has to do is look at the unregistered color images in the newspapers today to understand how even current technology has not resolved the registration perfectly and how peculiar someone's face will look when the eyes appear floating somewhere over the top of the head, or if a man's necktie is attached directly to his chin. Trade cards where the image is registered correctly, as well as cards with many colors show a higher degree of technical expertise on the part of the printmaker.

Perhaps because of the brilliant use of color, collecting trade cards and filling picture albums with them became a Victorian craze. Because so many of these cards were preserved in albums, it is not uncommon to find them today. However, intact albums command relatively high prices, and an individual would probably have been more interested in images than in collecting cards that advertised a certain type of business, so finding an album that consists solely of jewelry trade cards would be unlikely. While ephemera shows or the internet would be most productive sources for individual trade cards, you may find a few at flea markets and antiques shows, but it could be a time consuming process.

Nineteenth century jeweler's trade cards rarely give much insight into the kinds of jewelry that was being advertised. Occasionally one will find a description of the types of jewelry a company specialized in (see examples of trade cards), but generally all the information that's provided is the name of the company and the address. Sometimes the name of the city or town isn't even specified, as most of the jewelers were local and anyone who possessed a card would likely live in the same area.

Companies that produced trade cards had standard images for the local businessman to select from. Once the image was chosen, the name of the jeweler was printed in the spot left blank for that purpose. Some trade cards came in series (for example, there are as many as thirty-two cards produced by Boss Patented Watch Case Company in the Japanese style). Although some of the images may allude to the kinds of jewelry that a store carried (a man and a woman courting, for instance, may signify that the store sold wedding rings, or that the man may have greater success if he patronized a particular jeweler) it is rare to see depictions of jewelry itself.

Studying trade cards gives a collector greater insight into the era, and may enable one to document when a jeweler was in business. Some trade cards have copyright dates printed on them (generally the 1880s and 1890s). Comparing the style of the image to those reproduced in books on the subject may also help to date a card. Some of the cards are quite humorous; all of them reflect the styles and tastes of the time.

Trade cards that were designed reflecting the Japanese influence exemplify this point. After Commodore Perry established trade with Japan in the mid-1850s, the decorative arts of the Western world were greatly influenced by Japanese art. The imagery was new, and the Victorian loved novelty. The Japanese stressed craftsmanship and this appealed to those who were appalled at the machine made and sought to reinvestigate the merits of objects made by hand. Japanese artists didn't separate their work from their lives, and many Westerners saw this as virtuous and inspiring. Visionaries like Sigfried Bing recognized the power of Japanese arts and began both collecting and selling examples. The Centennial Exposition in Philadelphia, 1876, had a profound influence, as it marked the first exposure that vast numbers of Americans had to Japanese arts and crafts. The Japanese created an extensive exhibit and astonished Americans with the variety as well as the quality of the goods they displayed. There is a permanent exhibit at the Philadelphia Museum of Art which gives some sense of what was shown at the Centennial Exposition, and it is worth the trip there to see the authentic pavilion and some of the pieces that were actually shown in 1876. It is helpful to remember that Americans had no (or very little) exposure to this dramatically different artistic approach prior to end of Japanese isolation in 1853, as there had been no exchange between Japan and Western countries for centuries. A description from a book published in 1876 states, "Perhaps the greater part of the pleasure we receive in making the acquaintance of another nation is in the surprise it gives us, in the fillip our minds receive at being suddenly confronted with some utterly new and different ways of dealing with a familiar topic—some revelation of a thread-bare theme … It is not strange that the Japanese department was one of the main centres of attraction, and the delight of the curious and the bizarre, and at the same time the delicate and intricate workmanship." (Ingram, p. 559.) The Victorians were attracted to the subject matter and were intrigued by the outstanding craftsmanship. It offered an entirely new vocabulary, one based on standards the American's could appreciate and respect, one that incorporated humor, beauty, and tradition.

The trade cards illustrated here are wonderful examples of how American commercial artists took to these new images and design concepts. The cards sponsored by Boss Patented Watch Case Company were printed in light turquoise and black. They incorporated one of the elements that so appealed to the Victorian designer, the collage effect, where related but different patterns and designs were combined as if they had been cut out and assembled. (This effect was used extensively in the Aesthetic Movement.) The diaper pattern, where an image is repeated within a square, rectangular or diamond-shaped unit, is used in most examples. The designers also included images of Asian characters and things like bamboo fishing poles, owls, and fans, as well as a variety of typefaces, one of which was styled like Japanese calligraphy. Another characteristic that was emulated was the flattening of space (which particularly inspired the Impressionists). The typical Western device of linear perspective (parallel lines appear to converge at a point on the horizon) is not used consistently, but rather is merged with a new perspective which recognizes the picture plane as a flat surface, not necessarily emulating the effect of looking through a window. A clever addition is that each card includes a pocket watch as part of the image. In one case it may be used as the sun, in another it is the bait the man used to catch a gigantic fish, in another it's shown open and held over a man's head as an umbrella. One shows a rather hefty pig admiring his own reflection in the watch case. Again, the Victorian enjoyed humor and looked forward to the next variation, to discovering how the watch would be used in the next installment.

Another series of trade cards jewelers used to advertise their businesses included a young woman wearing colorful kimonos and platform sandals. She is shown in different activities on various cards, holding a bamboo umbrella walking in the rain, playing an accordion and singing, etc. She is shown in a Japanese garden, and the background is a solid gold color. The examples shown here were printed for a San Francisco firm that imported "rare and antique Oriental gems."

Another variation is a design that shows a scene from nature that appears to be painted with transparent watercolors (but is actually printed), with a patterned border. In this example, a fish spits water out of his spout-like mouth in order to catch an insect. The ways that the Japanese influence is seen in the trade cards is reflected in the jewelry of the era also, which follow.

Recommended Reading

Robert Alan Green, *Jewelers Trade Cards*.

Peter C. Marzio, *The Democratic Art: an Exhibition on the History of Chromolithography in America, 1840-1900*.

William Mosely, *The Japan Idea: Art and Life in Victorian America*.

Trade cards: Stowell & Company of Boston, circa 1860. Importers and retailers of clocks, bronze, silverware, and jewelry. Trade cards offer an intriguing peek at nineteenth century America. Not only do they describe the kinds of items that were sold, but they also offer a glimpse of popular culture. Also, the development of chromolithography led to a proliferation of advertising materials that were often collected and put into scrap books or albums in the 1800s. Because the images were so impressive to a public unfamiliar with color printing, they were often saved rather than discarded (despite their ephemeral quality). One of the largest holdings of American trade cards and business ephemera is the Warshaw Collection at the Museum of American History in Washington, D.C. This is an early trade card, one that predates the use of color. Values for cards range from $5-$50.

Chromolithograph trade card, A. J. Robinson & Co., watches and diamonds, jewelry and silverware, circa 1880.

Chromolithograph trade card, Cahoone, Alexander & Co., of Providence, Rhode Island. "Dealers in Diamonds Manufacturers and Repairers of all Kinds of Solid Gold Jewelry." Circa 1880. Good luck horse shoe embellished with roses and forget-me-nots. Symbols for good luck were frequently used in jewelry, and there was an entire lexicon of the language of flowers.

Chromolithograph trade card, Orton the Jeweler, Canastota, New York, 1883, by Ed Wolf. Silver background, rose colored ink on figures. Scene of a man and woman having a conversation. The milkmaid is carrying her stool and bucket, the gentleman carries his gloves and walking stick.

Chromolithograph trade card, Stillman & Hitchcock, Jewelers, Canastota, circa 1880. Vase with red roses.

Chromolithograph trade card, Orton the Jeweler, Canastota, New York, circa 1880. Blue ladies slipper with daisies.

Chromolithograph trade card, O'Brien's manufacturer of ornamental hair work, as well as wigs and curls. Youths as fairies with tiny wings on a branch with apple blossoms and a butterfly with multicolored wings. Circa 1880.

Chromolithograph trade card, F. H. Kramer, "Cheapest high grade Jewelry house in the city." Young girl is pulling two boys in a wagon.

Chromolithograph trade card, Jeweler. Gold background, young woman wearing a dress and hat made of pansies reaching for a letter being delivered by a dove. Circa 1880.

Chromolithograph trade card, Henry Rowlands, jeweler and importer, Albany, New York. Baby paddles a lily pad amongst the reeds. Gold background.

Chromolithograph trade card, G. T. Marsh & Co., "importers of rare and antique Oriental gems." Girl wearing a kimono, walking through a puddle wearing platform sandals, holding an umbrella. In the Japanese style, circa 1880.

Chromolithograph trade card, G. T. Marsh & Co., "importers of rare and antique Oriental gems." Girls wearing a kimono, playing an accordion. In the Japanese style, circa 1880.

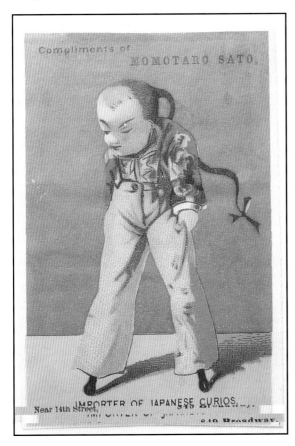

Chromolithograph trade card, Momotaro Sato, "Importer of Japanese Curios." Boy with long queue walking on stilts, gold background. In the Japanese style, circa 1880.

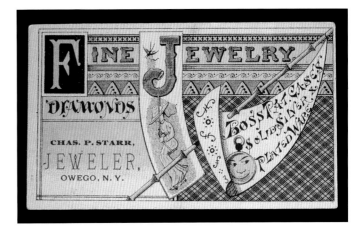

Chromolithograph trade card, Boss Watches. In the Japanese/aesthetic style, with diaper pattern, collage effect. Chas. P. Star, Jeweler, Owego, New York, circa 1880.

Chromolithograph trade card, Boss Watches. In the Japanese/aesthetic style, with diaper pattern, collage effect, with man catching a large fish with a block and tackle. Henry Rogers, Jeweler, Sabula, Iowa. Circa 1880.

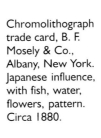

Chromolithograph trade card, B. F. Mosely & Co., Albany, New York. Japanese influence, with fish, water, flowers, pattern. Circa 1880.

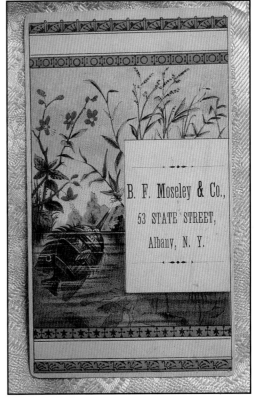

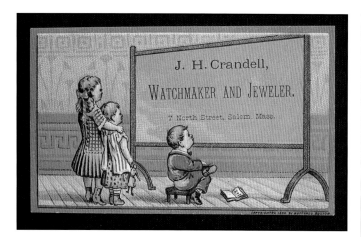

Chromolithograph trade card, "J. H. Crandell, watchmaker and jeweler, 7 North Street, Salem, Mass." Young children look at the information as if it is written on a portable black board.

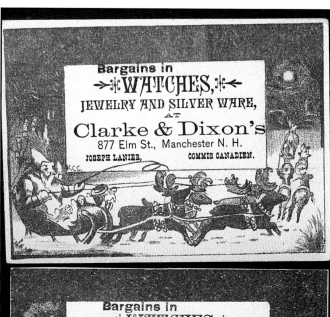

Continued: St. Nicholas and reindeer, two men carrying sign, but the second man is distracted by a dog nipping at his backside. Humor also helps us to see our ancestors as real people, people who experienced life, who laughed at silly things, and who kept on going.

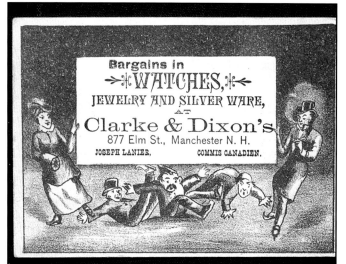

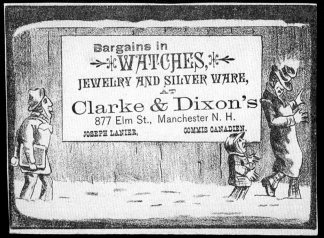

Chromolithograph trade card, "Bargains in Watches, Jewelry and Silver Ware, Clarke & Dixon's, 877 Elm Street, Manchester, New Hampshire." Four trade cards with humorous winter scenes: two skaters holding sign while three skaters fall on the ice, and people walking in the snow and the first man is jolted by a pile of snow falling on his head.

Chromolithograph trade card, "H. W. Appleton, Watches and Jewelry, Repairing of Fine Watches a Specialty. 884 Third Avenue, New York."

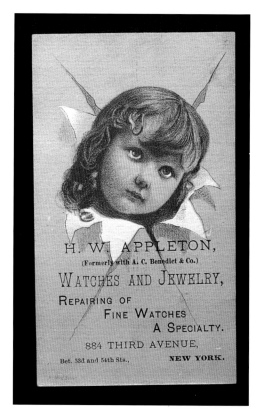

Japanese Influence

Scarf ring in two colored gold, in the Japanese style. While this scarf pin is not marked, it is virtually identical to the jewelry designed by Edward C. Moore for Tiffany (see Loring, 2003, page 26). Circa 1870. $450-$525.

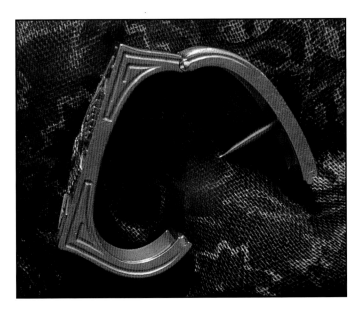

Scarf ring opened.

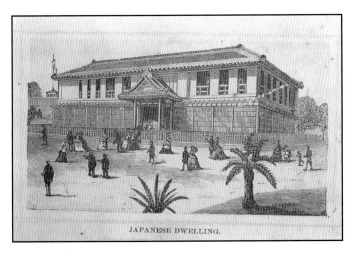

"Japanese Dwelling" at the Centennial Exposition in Philadelphia, 1876. There is an excellent exhibit at the Philadelphia Museum of Art that shows many of the objects that were displayed during the Centennial Exposition, as well as a few of the actual buildings.

Cover of *Japonica*, published in 1891.

Stereographic view, circa 1890, with Mt. Fuji appearing above the clouds.

Detail of platter in the Japanese style, circa 1880. Marked "B. D. & Co., Warwick." $150-$175. *Courtesy of Giselle De Rienzo Antiques.*

Chromolithograph of a Western woman in a kimono, holding a fan, circa 1870.

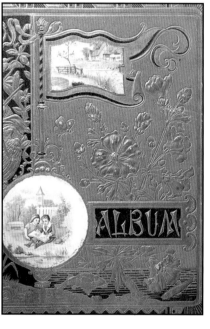

Cover of a scrap book from the 1890s, in the Japanese style.

Japanese designs with fish and shrimp, from *Étoffes de Soie du Japon*, plate 19 (H. Ernst, Editeur, Paris, n.d., but circa 1880).

Cover of book entitled *The Land of the Almighty Dollar*. (See page 86.)

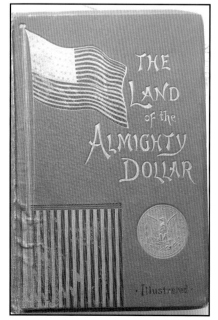

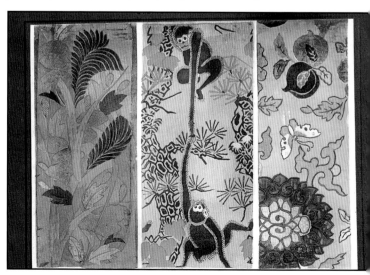

Japanese designs, from *Étoffes de Soie du Japon*, plate 19.

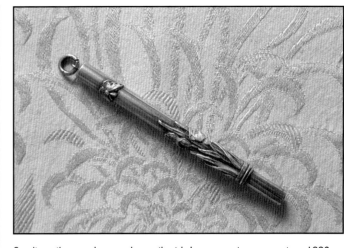

Sterling silver and enamel pencil with Japanese signature, circa 1890. $475-$550.

Vest pocket pencil, sterling silver and enamel with "HICKS" mark. $500-$600. *Courtesy of John McKenzie.*

Vest pocket pencil. Tropical foliage, not marked. $500-$600. *Courtesy of John McKenzie.*

Magic pencil in the form of Okame, goddess of mirth (with a male figure on the reverse). Made by Edward Todd & Co., circa 1880. Mixed metals, 1 1/4" x 1/2". $950-$1,200.

Two vest pocket pencils. Owl with crescent moon on one side and love birds kissing on the other. Hallmarked. *Courtesy of John McKenzie.* $300-$400 each.

Magic pencil in the form of a Buddha, marked, circa 1880. N.P.

Japanese sterling silver and enamel brooch with a crane and kappa (a mythological water creature). 2", circa 1870. $375-$450.

Loft's candy tin, circa 1910. Crane and kappa imagery similar to that on sterling silver brooch.

Two sterling silver belt buckles, marked "Shiebler." In the Japanese style, with sea horses, beetles, fish, etc. *Courtesy of Rachel Marks Antiques.* $900-$1050.

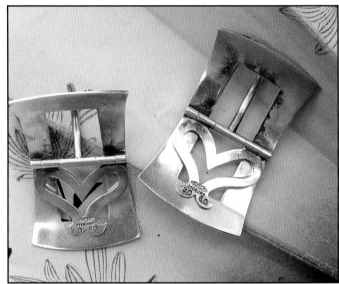

Reverse view of preceding photograph, with Shiebler mark.

Shiebler brooch, with applied crane and palm fronds, hand engraved Japanese characters. Circa 1890. $675-$750. *Courtesy of Rachel Marks Antiques.*

Appliqué and enamel sterling silver brooch (with birds and flowers). *Courtesy of Rachel Marks Antiques.*

Sterling silver brooch, circa 1880. (This brooch is dented. Many of these brooches and lockets are light weight and can be easily dented. Some repairs are fairly easy to make, if the back is open and if the area that needs to be repaired is uncomplicated. However, many noses of Art Nouveau ladies are indented and that is difficult to repair, especially if the metal has broken through.) $35-$55.

Sterling silver Victorian brooch with hand engraved and applied gold basket and apple blossoms. $175-$225. Right: Sterling silver brooch/locket, circa 1880. $135-$185. *Courtesy of Rachel Marks Antiques.*

Oval brooch, sterling silver, circa 1880. 1 1/4" x 1", $35-$55.

This view shows the locket on the right open, with the motto "Forget me not" inside.

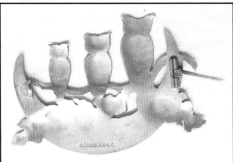

Reverse of preceding photograph.

Brooch with three owls sitting on an oak branch, with a crescent moon. Hand engraved, pierced design. Inscribed "K. O. P. 1890." The maker is "M. S. Cooler, N. D." $150-$185. *Courtesy of Rachel Marks Antiques.*

"Shiebler" medallion brooch. $575-$650. *Courtesy of Rachel Marks Antiques.*

"Shiebler" brooch, with four overlapping square medallions, circa 1890. Sterling silver, $575-$650. *Courtesy of Rachel Marks Antiques.*

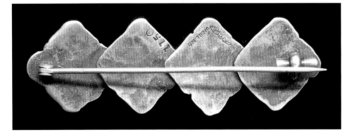

Reverse of above.

Brooch made of silver plated metal, with medallions. Compared to the Shiebler brooches, it is clearly not as well made, not as interesting. All the profiles are the same, with the exception of the face on the round drop medallion. The medallions are die stamped to give the appearance of having been hand-forged and the plated metal is thinner that the sterling silver stock used in the Shiebler pieces. $45-$75.

"Shiebler" medallion brooch, sterling silver, 1 3/4" round, with beading around the circumference. $575-$650. *Courtesy of Rachel Marks Antiques.*

Art Nouveau brooch, sterling silver, 1 3/4". Art Nouveau brooches range in value from $350-$900. Pictured brooch: $450-$525. *Courtesy of Rachel Marks Antiques.*

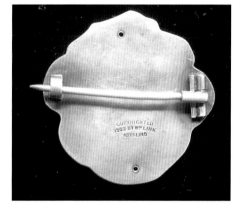

Reverse of previous photograph, with maker's mark: Link, copyrighted 1902.

Art Nouveau brooch. *Courtesy of Rachel Marks Antiques.* N.P.

Reverse of Art Nouveau brooch. *Courtesy of Rachel Marks Antiques.*

Art Nouveau brooch. *Courtesy of Rachel Marks Antiques.*

Art Nouveau brooch. *Courtesy of Rachel Marks Antiques.* $765-$825. Larger Art Nouveau brooches, 2" and more, range from $600-$1200.

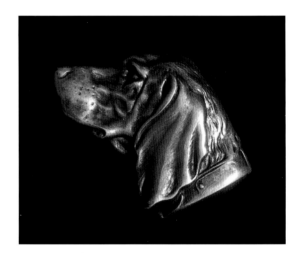

Dog head. $75-$150. Brooch signed Unger Bros. 1".

Art Nouveau brooch. *Courtesy of Rachel Marks Antiques.*

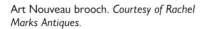

Art Nouveau brooch. *Courtesy of Rachel Marks Antiques.*

Art Nouveau brooch. Marked "La Pierre." $425-$525. *Courtesy of Rachel Marks Antiques.*

Art Nouveau brooch. Marked "Kerr." 2 3/4" x 1 3/4". $625-$675. *Courtesy of Rachel Marks Antiques.*

"Heinz" brooch, with flowers and leaves (sterling silver on patinated copper). $450-$550. *Courtesy of Rachel Marks Antiques.*

Epitome of the Art Nouveau style, this brooch/chatelaine holder is made of 14 kt. gold with bezel-set, faceted rubies and plique a jour. The "butterfly woman" was an image distinctly Art Nouveau. $2,200-$2,350. *Courtesy of Adele Golden, The Garden Gate Antiques.*

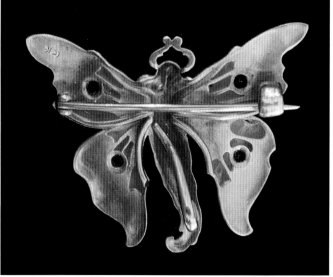

Reverse of the brooch in the previous photograph. Note the open bezels, as well as the pierced design that allows light to shine through the transparent and translucent enamel.

"Heinz "brooch, with symmetrical composition of flowers and leaves. $450-$550. *Courtesy of Rachel Marks Antiques.*

From Kate Greenaway book.

"Shiebler" Homeric brooch, sterling silver. $650-$750. *Courtesy of Rachel Marks Antiques.*

Kerr pin #1353. Silver with gold wash. $385-$450. *Courtesy of Rachel Marks Antiques.*

Kate Greenaway girl playing tennis. Unmarked, sterling silver. 2" x 1". $125-$175. *Courtesy of Rachel Marks Antiques.*

Kerr chatelaine holder. 2" x 1". $125-$145. *Courtesy of Rachel Marks Antiques.*

Girl with hat.
Sterling silver.
$75-$125.

Stick pin. Sterling silver.
$75-$125.

Flowers. Poppies and branch, sterling silver. 2 1/2" x 2". $175-$225.
Courtesy of Rachel Marks Antiques.

Flowers. Kerr
jonquil and
branch. $295-
$355. *Courtesy of
Rachel Marks
Antiques.*

Snowflake. Sterling silver. Arts & Crafts. $75-$95.
Courtesy of Rachel Marks Antiques.

Reverse of
previous image.

Lily pad brooch.
*Courtesy of Rachel
Marks Antiques.*

Flower. Kerr flower and branch. $185-$285. *Courtesy of Rachel Marks Antiques.*

Bicycle. Die stamped sterling. $30-$50.

Basket of flowers brooch, signed "CINI," sterling silver with gold wash. $148-$175. *Courtesy of Rachel Marks Antiques.*

African figure. Sterling silver. 2" x 2". $225-$300.

Reverse of basket of flowers.

Reverse of African figure.

Feather brooches, circa. 1940. Several by Beau.

Feather.

Feather.

Backs of feather brooches.

Sterling silver brooch.

Sterling silver flowers with red glass stone centers pin, circa 1940.

Marked "H.I. 1/20 12 kt gf." Two circles with flowers, leaves, tendrils, and ribbons, two-toned gold filled with green stones. Circa 1950. $15-$35.

Sterling silver, stylized leaves and tendril. Circa 1940.

Marquise and round faceted opaque turquoise colored glass stones and white metal brooch, abstract flower motif, circa 1950. $35-$45.

Horse brooch, cast in silver. Signed "Guglielmo Cini." Circa 1945. $75-$95.

Brooch with repoussè flowers and leaves. Signed "Sterling Craft by Coro." Circa 1945, $65-$85.

Sterling silver basket of flowers. Pin and earrings. Circa. 1940. $35-$150.

Sterling silver flower and earrings.

Sterling silver blue glass center in center of flower.

Three sterling silver flowers with clear rhinestone centers.

Sterling silver flowers.

Sterling silver flowers.

Gold filled brooch.

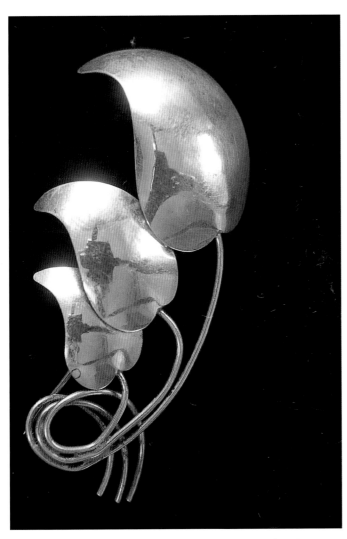

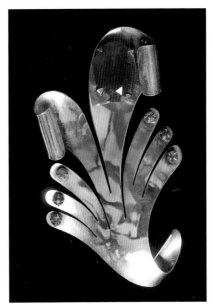

Large sterling silver brooch, circa 1940. 4". $75-$125.

Sterling silver. Retro style broach with green cabachones. Circa 1940. $175-$250.

Sterling silver brooch, three graduated, stylized leaves. $25-$35.

Another retro sterling silver with gold wash brooch, possibly made by Mazer. $175-$250.

Sterling silver bow brooch, with large red glass emerald-cut stone. Circa 1940, $125-$150. *Courtesy Vita Materasso.*

Retro sterling silver pin I was wearing when I met jewelry designer Larry Vrba, on which he commented. $225-$325.

Sterling silver with gold wash bouquet of flowers secured with a bow, trembler. Circa 1940, $175-$225.

Vermeil brooch made by Napier. $35-$55.

Vermeil brooch made by Napier. $35-$55..

Two sterling silver parrots, with glass stone eyes. Circa 1940. $75-$95.

Reverse of the pin with Jazz musicians.

Silver and enamel pin with Jazz musicians. English hallmarks. *Private collection.* N.P. (**no p**rice).

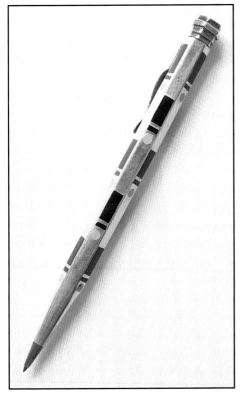

Art Deco pencil, made of sterling silver with inlaid black and turquoise enamel. Circa 1930, $225-$250.

Tiffany pin with a duck. *Courtesy of Rachel Marks Antiques.* $265-$325.

Jensen heart, sterling silver. $150-$250.

Reverse of Jensen heart.

Sterling silver pin with trees and water. *Courtesy Rachel Marks Antiques.*

Jensen pin. $450-$525. *Courtesy Rachel Marks Antiques.*

Jensen pin. $450-$525. *Courtesy Rachel Marks Antiques.*

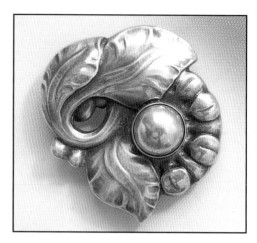

Jensen Brooch. *Courtesy Rachel Marks Antiques.*

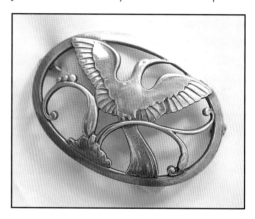

Sterling silver brooch, signed "Jensen, #238." Bird (of Paradise?) and stylized branches. $450-$550. *Courtesy Rachel Marks Antiques.*

Reverse of above, showing markings. *Courtesy Rachel Marks Antiques.*

Pin with stylized leaves marked 925. $85-$125. *Courtesy Rachel Marks Antiques.*

Hecho in Mexico. Made in Mexico. *Courtesy of Gerald Schultz, The Antique Gallery.* $45-$65.

Lily pad bracelet. Danecraft, circa 1940. $45-$65.

Detail showing maker's mark (or, in jewelry collecting parlance, signature).

Jensen bracelet. Sterling with gold wash and chrysophase. $1400-$1600. *Courtesy of Rachel Marks Antiques.*

Sterling silver Art Nouveau bracelet. $175-$250. *Courtesy of Rachel Marks Antiques.*

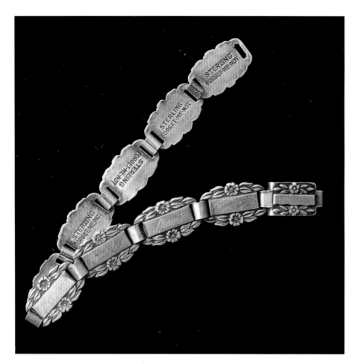

Sterling silver forget-me-not bracelet. Range from $125-$325. *Courtesy of Rachel Marks Antiques.*

Cuff bracelet. Range from $125-$325. *Courtesy of Rachel Marks Antiques.*

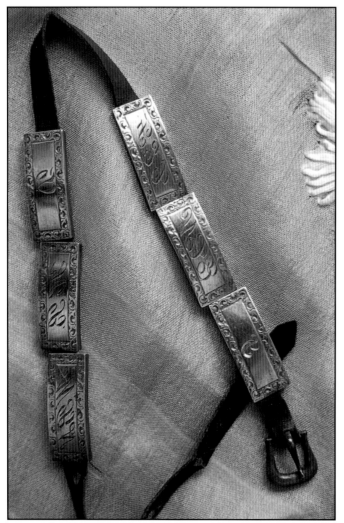

Nineteenth century friendship bracelet.

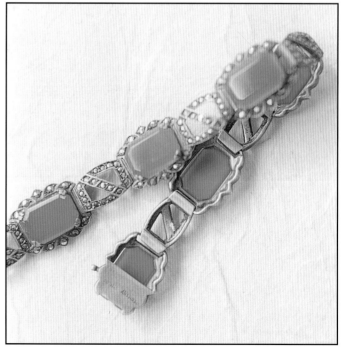

Bracelet. Range from $125-$325. *Courtesy of Rachel Marks Antiques.*

Research

*P*art of the adventure of collecting is the process of learning more about whatever one collects. Initially, most of us start collecting because something catches our eye. It reminds us of our childhood, or brings to mind fond memories of an event which took place earlier in our lives. It could be because of an association, a family connection or because the objects are somehow connected to our work, hobby, or other interests. The connection may not even be apparent until some later date, when you realize you've been collecting depression glass because of a story once told by your grandmother.

History

Studying jewelry by referencing art history is helpful. For example, *Metropolitan Jewelry* is an interesting book to refer to, as it has great illustrations of both paintings and actual, historic jewelry that's housed in the Metropolitan Museum of Art. Studying jewelry in museum permanent collections as well as the jewelry in special exhibits (like the exhibit of Treasures of the World at the Met) is especially rewarding — the only problem is that none of it is for sale!

Recommended Reading

Vivienne Becker, *Antique and Twentieth Century Jewelry*.
C. Jeannenne Bell, *Answers to Questions About Old Jewelry, 1840-1950*.
Martha Gandy Fales, *Jewelry in America, 1600-1900*.
Sally Everitt and David Lancaster, *Christie's Twentieth-Century Jewelry*.
Clare Phillips, *Jewelry From Antiquity to the Present*.
Christine Romero, *Warman's Jewelry, 1st, 2nd, 3rd Editions*.

Primary Sources

Photographs, Ephemera, Etc.

*P*rimary sources are probably the best way to learn directly, without the interference of someone else's theories or synopsis.

There are many original sources to consult. Old newspapers and magazines, dictionaries, encyclopedias, compendiums, catalogues, broadsides, and trade cards can be invaluable sources for information. Examining old photographs provides an excellent opportunity to use your observational skills to test theories and to come to your own conclusions, which you will be able to document by the photographs themselves. It's an adventure, as you never know what you'll find. For example, you may read that a particular style of jewelry is prevalent during a certain time period. Yet you may find a photograph that shows someone wearing a piece of that jewelry almost fifty years after the style had gone out of fashion.

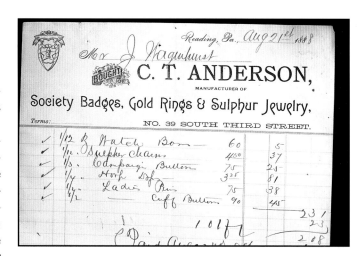

"C. T. Anderson, Manufacturers of Society Badges, Gold Rings and Sulphur Jewelry." Dated August 21, 1888, this billhead indicates costs of "sulphur chains" and campaign buttons. It is likely that what's described as sulphur jewelry was black hard rubber, or vulcanite, jewelry, which was stabilized with sulphur.

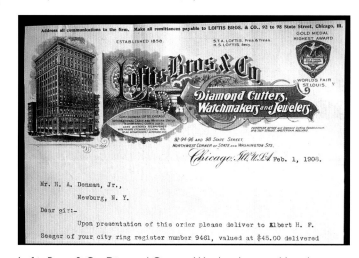

Loftis Bros. & Co. Diamond Cutters, Watchmakers, and Jewelers from Chicago, Illinois. February 1, 1908. The elegant handwriting of the Tiffany document is now replaced by a typewriter. This billhead includes an engraving of the building that housed the Loftis Brothers business.

Letterheads, bills, and receipts can also shed light on the customs, practices, styles, and economics of the past. The design of the logo, addresses, the items that are described, the prices, and even the handwriting or typewriter font help us gain a clearer understanding of the past. This example is from Tiffany & Co., Union Square, New York. In 1882, Tiffany is described and an "importer of diamonds, precious stones, jewelry, bronzes, clocks, fine porcelain, glass and stationary," as well as "manufacturers of jewelry, watches, silver and plated ware."

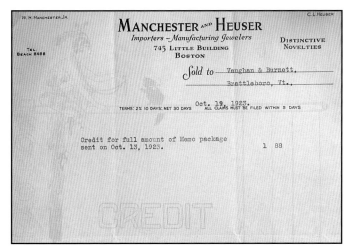

"Manchester and Heuser, Importers, Manufacturing Jewelers, Distinctive Novelties," October 1923. Although this billhead doesn't tell us much about the goods produced by Manchester and Heuser, the discrete image of the flapper enticing a kitten with her pearl Sautior. She is wearing an aigrette on her forehead, a form-fitting sheath with a long train, and a peacock feather design; the kitten is wearing a suitably formal black coat and bow.

Cartier advertising calendar, 1958. With line drawings of Cartier shops. Again, ephemera is critically helpful in learning more about the companies that manufactured or sold jewelry. Here we see what Cartier storefronts looked like in the 1950s. $25-$45.

Advertising card with ring measurements from Baird North, Gold and Silversmiths, Providence, Rhode Island. Circa 1910.

Celluloid advertising mirror/pin holder (around perimeter), with birthstones of the month. 2", circa 1910. $25-$45.

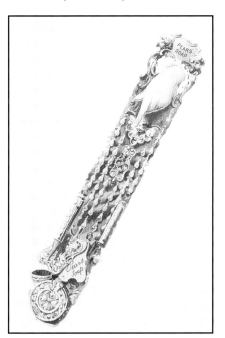

Pear's Soap advertisement/bookmark with silver chatelaine holding a retractable pencil, a pin holder, and thimble. Circa 1890. $35-$50.

Celluloid advertising mirror with stones of the month. $25-$45.

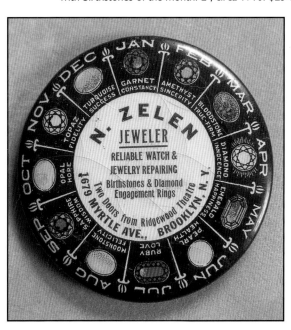

"Diamond and Gold Jewelry" *Demorest's Monthly Magazine*, January 1878. The crosses, which could be worn as a necklace or brooch, are ornamented with up to eleven diamonds, and the price would vary depending on the quality of the gems ($150-$400). The earrings were set with fifteen diamonds and colored gold, and cost $75 in 1878.

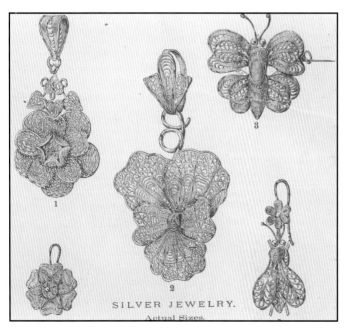

Silver jewelry (*Demorest's Monthly Magazine*, January 1878, page 33): "Silver jewelry is now in unusual favor, not only by reason of comparative novelty, but also because, as at present designed, it is really so pretty."

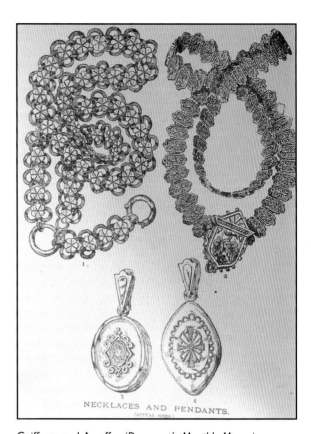

Coiffures and Agraffes (*Demorest's Monthly Magazine*, January 1878, page 34): Agraffes were used to fasten cloaks. The examples shown here are in the Japanese style, "very novel and stylish."

Bracelets and pendants in rolled gold. (*Demorest's Monthly Magazine*, May 1878, page 266.)

Brooches and earrings, "Handsome and novel in design, this set of scarf-pin and earrings is of 'rolled gold.' The body is of dead gold, tastefully ornamented with filigree work, the raised bars and balls are burnished. Price $4.50." (*Demorest's Monthly Magazine*, June 1878, page 322.)

Ladies' necklaces and pendants. (*Demorest's Monthly Magazine*, December 1878, page 669.)

Victorian locket on a book chain. Locket is made of silver with Bohemian garnet and turquoise cabochons, $450-$650. *Courtesy of Ruth Taylor*.

Brooches and earrings. (*Demorest's Monthly Magazine*, August 1878, page 434.)

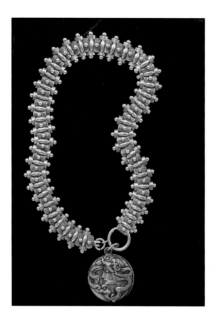

Victorian book chain with later, Art Nouveau locket (locket is plated). $400-$550. *Courtesy of Ruth Taylor*.

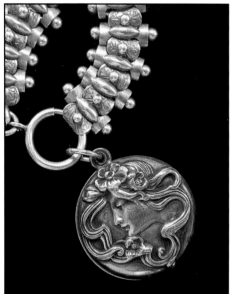

Detail of above.

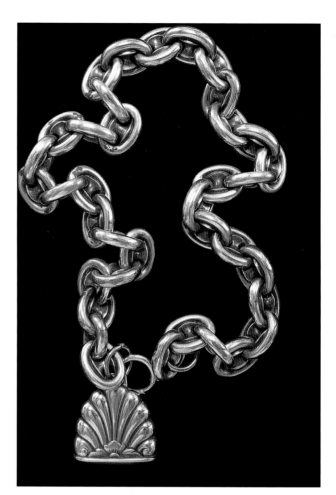

"Slave chain" 14" link chain with fob. $400-$600. *Courtesy of Ruth Taylor*.

Photograph advertising Art Nouveau jewelry and silver novelties offered by C. D. Peacock of Chicago, from *The Cosmopolitan*, December 1903.

Locket in gold and silver. $160-$225.

Photographs

History of Photography

*A*nother way to add to a collection of jewelry is through acquiring photographs of people wearing jewelry. This type of collection would evolve fairly quickly, as there are multitudes of early photographs still available at flea markets and antiques shows. Again, it would be logical to have a particular starting point, perhaps nineteenth century photographs of women, limited to one-of-a-kind tintypes or photographs on paper that were printed from negatives.

It's important to try to read through the eyes of a nineteenth century citizen. If you can be objective, you'll learn more. You'll find valuable the ability to read and interpret the clues found in your photographs, such as that a photograph may be printed on a cabinet card that dates to 1870, but that the styles indicate a much earlier date. Assessing the clues, you could jump to the conclusion that the style started earlier, or you could realize that photographers used whatever stock they had, and if they had left-over materials that needed to be used, they would use them, even ten years later.

Studying Nineteenth Century Photographs

The invention of photography was made public in 1839. By the 1850s, photography was accepted as a means of preserving images of family and friends and was accessible to many more people than painted portraits had ever been. The Daguerreotype was the first type of photograph that was widely available, and was aptly called the "mirror with a memory" because the image was created on the mirror-like surface of a silver-plated copper plate. Tintypes were also photographs on a metal plate, but they weren't available until 1850.

By studying the actual photographs one can learn what kinds of jewelry was worn and how it was worn. For example, it surprised me that so many women wore watch chains. Also, the size of the jewelry was often unlike what I had anticipated. So much of the nineteenth century jewelry we see for sale at antiques shows is relatively delicate, yet many of the women in photographs wear large chains and pendants (especially crosses). Many women wore both a brooch and a necklace simultaneously. While it is possible that in the earlier days of photography people wore all their finery when they posed, by the 1880s photography was common enough that it is likely that, while people dressed nicely to be photographed, they didn't feel the need to wear every jewel they owned.

In order to ascertain when a particular style of jewelry was worn, it helps to have some background in both the history of photography and the history of fashion in nineteenth century America.

Recommended Reading

Priscilla Harris Dalrymple, *American Victorian Costume in Early Photographs*.

Alison Gernsheim, *Victorian and Edwardian Fashion, a Photographic Survey*.

O. Henry Mace, *Collector's Guide to Early Photographs*.

The invention of photography in 1829 led to an unprecedented opportunity. We now have the ability to study how the middle classes, as well as the upper classes, dressed, the jewelry they wore, etc. Hand tinted tintype of a young woman wearing drop earrings and a black beaded necklace (probably made of jet). Unmarked photo, circa 1865. 1 1/2" (1/6 plate) image fit into an oval, embossed carte de visite.

Tintype of four young women and a young man. Two of the women wear earrings, two wear necklaces (one with a book chain and drop with a locket), one woman wears a bangle bracelet. Unmarked photo, circa 1860, 1/6 plate.

Tintype of a woman wearing a brooch. 2 1/2" x 3 1/4" (1/6 plate), circa 1860.

Calotype of a young woman wearing drop earrings and a brooch at her collar, circa 1870. Also wearing a choker with a heart drop. Unmarked photo.

Hand tinted tintype of a woman wearing gold earrings and a gold brooch. Unmarked, circa 1865.

Carte de visite, with a woman wearing earrings, wide chain with a locket. Photo marked A. Wheeler, Unadilla, New York. Circa 1870.

Carte de visite of a young woman wearing a velvet choker and brooch, circa 1870. Photo marked S. Towle Photographer, No. 92 Merrimack Street, Lowell, Massachusetts.

Carte de visite of a woman wearing drop earrings, bar pin at the neckline and a book chain with a drop and large cross. Circa 1870. Photo marked G. A. Ellis, Photographer, Richmond, Michigan.

Carte de visite of a woman wearing a triple strand of jet beads with a large cross and heavy, carved jet drop earrings. Photo marked "Mrs. Fanny French, 1876" E. Decker Photographer, 243 Superior Street, Cleveland, Ohio.

Carte de visite of a woman wearing a brooch and watch chain at her waist. Circa 1870.

Carte de visite of a woman holding a fan, wearing a watch chain at her waist. Circa 1870.

Cabinet card portrait of a woman wearing stud earrings in pierced ears, with an Albert chain and a gun-shaped charm (possibly a watch key or magic pencil), watch tucked into the trim of her dress. Photo marked Oakleys Cottage Studio, circa 1880.

Cabinet card of a young woman wearing drop earrings, a large brooch, book chain (without a drop), and a pendant, wedding band, and bangles on her wrists. One of the bracelets is shaped like a belt and buckle. Circa 1880. Photo marked Fromley, Newton, New Jersey.

Cabinet card of a young woman wearing a watch chain, brooch, and hair ornament. Photograph by Lee, South Main Street, N.J., circa 1880.

Cabinet card of a woman wearing wire rim glasses and a micro-mosaic brooch depicting the Roman Coliseum. Photo marked Semple & Stein Photographers, 67 North Pearl Street, Albany, New York. Circa 1880.

Cabinet card of a woman with a chain and fob, and a stick pin at the collar, with rustic scenery. Photograph by Bowers, 135 North Main Street, Concord, New Hampshire. Circa 1880.

Cabinet card of a young woman wearing a watch chain and a brooch with a name. Unmarked, circa 1880.

Cabinet card of a young woman wearing a brooch in the shape of a scimitar (Shriner emblem), with a chain hanging from it. Photo marked Hudson and Shadle, Algona, Iowa. Circa 1880.

Cabinet card of a young woman wearing a watch chain. Circa 1880. Photographer's name has been removed.

Cabinet card of a young woman wearing a brooch with a hanging chain and charm (Shriner emblem). The young women in these two photographs are wearing the same pattern dress, and are probably sisters, as sisters often wore similar or identical dresses in photographs. Photo marked Hudson and Shadle, Algona, Iowa. Circa 1880.

Shriner emblem, in silver and abalone. Approximately 1", $25-$35.

Cabinet card of Alice E. Cummings wearing a watch chain with a charm, the watch tucked into the lace trim of the dress. Photograph by Justin Halmrash, 529 Washington Ave. South, Minneapolis. Circa 1880.

Cabinet card of a young woman (Flora Smith?), with drop earrings in the shape of crowns with white gem pendants. She is also wearing a bar pin at her rushed lace neckline. Photo marked Rabineau Photographic Art Studio, 9 & 11 Pearl St., Troy, New York. Circa 1880.

Family portrait (Adrian Pinney and wife), mother is wearing a silver belt buckle. Circa 1890, unmarked photograph.

Women wearing small brooches. The woman in the foreground has a brooch in the shape of a pansy. Circa 1890. Unmarked photograph.

Photograph of two young women in a stylized pose. Both have large ribbons in their hair. One is wearing a cameo, the other is wearing a brooch with a photograph in it. It's helpful when an example of a particular type of jewelry is found within a photograph. Photograph by Freeland, Milford, New Jersey. Circa 1890. 1 3/4" x 2 1/2".

Oval photograph of a young woman in a big hat, with a silver belt buckle and ring. Circa 1890, unmarked.

Silver with gold wash brooch with tintype, beveled glass. $125-$175. *Courtesy Adele Golden of The Garden Gate Antiques, Philadelphia.*

Cabinet card of a young woman with a velvet choker, circa 1890. Photograph by Hartford, 376 Broadway, Boston.

Photograph in heart-shaped pin, circa 1910. $35-$50.

Postcard (3" x 5") of a young woman with a large hat, fur coat, and muff. She's wearing a locket, stud earrings, and a very long hat pin. Circa 1900.

Oval photograph (3 1/2" x 2 1/2") of two young women, one wearing a double chain and locket. Circa 1900, photograph by Norman, 39 1/2 Cony St., August, Maine.

Young woman with an upswept hairdo, wearing pince-nez, two bar pins, and chain, circa 1900. Unmarked.

Oval photograph (4" x 6 1/2") of young woman with long hair, wearing a chain. Circa 1910, unmarked.

Photograph (5 1/2" x 4") of a woman wearing a beaded dress with a long, draped chain and multithreaded pearl choker with pendant. Circa 1910. Photograph by Gray, 1030 Tremont St., Boston. Inscribed "In memory of 'Maplecroft' Alice Cora Wood."

Photograph of a woman wearing a brooch made of woven hair. Although the style of jewelry dates much earlier, this appears to be a photograph taken in the early 1900s. Merrill Photo.

Family photographs also contribute to our understanding of jewelry, about the individuals who wore it, and the lives they led. Following are examples of photographs and jewelry that were inherited by one individual. Here we see a portrait of Beverly Houghton's grandmother (Jeanette Dickerson, "Nettie") and her siblings (Harry Estil, Olivia, and Clarence Dickerson). Circa 1890, Vorhees and Devoe Photographers, Dallas, Texas. The following items have no price as they are part of a private collection. N.P. *Courtesy of Beverly Houghton.*

Postcard of a young woman with a very large white bow, a pendant, and bangle bracelet. Inscribed "Ask Uncle Cal if this looks like the baby that used to come to meet him when the whistle blew. Arvila K. Niece." Circa 1910. N.P. *Courtesy of Beverly Houghton.*

Sunday School attendance medal, awarded to Nettie in 1897. N.P. *Courtesy of Beverly Houghton.*

Cameo of a woman wearing pendant earrings. With prong-set garnets, worn as a brooch or pendant, owned by Nettie. 1" x 1 1/4". N.P. *Courtesy of Beverly Houghton.*

Cameo of a woman with a flower in her hair, wearing a miniature emerald necklace, silver filigree marked sterling, approx. 1" x 1 1/4", owned by Nettie, circa 1910. N.P. *Courtesy of Beverly Houghton.*

Cameo ring with enameled gold band, circa 1910. N.P. *Courtesy of Beverly Houghton.*

Signet ring, Julius Ernest Foreman, 1884-1942. N.P. *Courtesy of Beverly Houghton.*

Silver brooch in the Japanese style, with bird on a branch, diaper pattern, and crenellated border. Approx 1 1/2", circa 1880. N.P. *Courtesy of Beverly Houghton.*

Reverse view of the silver brooch. N.P. *Courtesy of Beverly Houghton.*

Gold bracelets owned by Jeanette Dickerson Foreman, 1/2" wide and 5/8" wide (inscribed "Nettie"). N.P. *Courtesy of Beverly Houghton.*

Gold pocket watch given to Nettie by Julius Foreman as a wedding present. Elgin, 14 kt. gold, 15 jewels, number 11501281, circa 1905. N.P. *Courtesy of Beverly Houghton.*

Watch open. N.P. *Courtesy of Beverly Houghton.*

Marks on watch. N.P. *Courtesy of Beverly Houghton.*

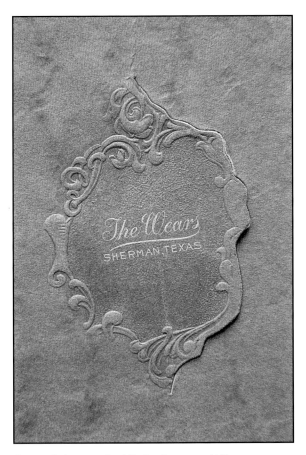

Cover of photograph of Evelyn Foreman. N.P.
Courtesy of Beverly Houghton.

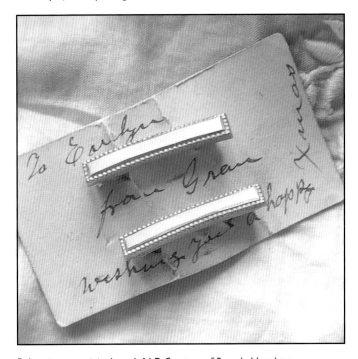

Gold bar pin worn by Evelyn in the previous photograph. N.P.
Courtesy of Beverly Houghton.

Baby pins on original card. N.P. *Courtesy of Beverly Houghton.*

Photograph of Evelyn Foreman
wearing a gold bar pin. N.P.
Courtesy of Beverly Houghton.

Gold heart necklace. N.P. *Courtesy of Beverly Houghton.*

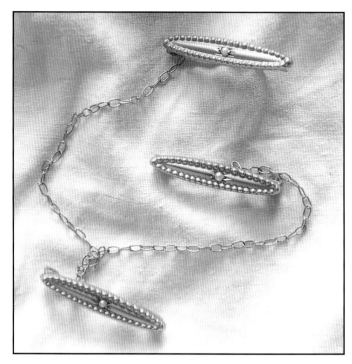

Three gold baby pins with tiny chain linking them. N.P. *Courtesy of Beverly Houghton.*

Reverse of gold heart necklace. N.P. *Courtesy of Beverly Houghton.*

Brass jewelry box. N.P. *Courtesy of Beverly Houghton.*

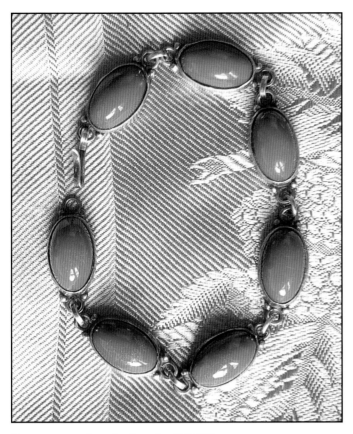

Green stone and sterling bracelet. $50-$75.

Detail showing maker's mark of Ballesteros, a Mexican maker.

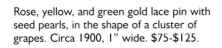

Rose, yellow, and green gold lace pin with seed pearls, in the shape of a cluster of grapes. Circa 1900, 1" wide. $75-$125.

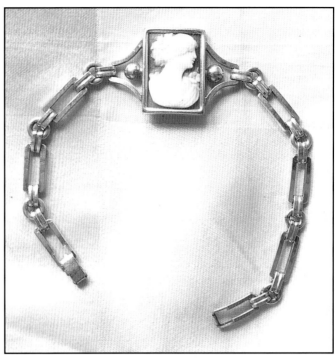

Cameo bracelet, signed Simonds.

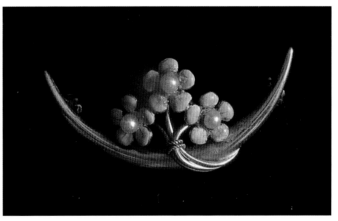

Gold crescent pin with pale blue enameled forget-me-nots. Circa 1900, $75-$125.

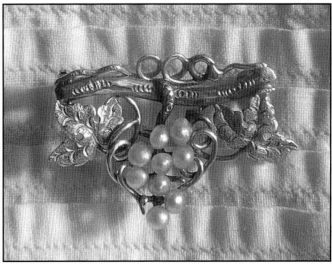

Pearls. No prices this page. *Courtesy of the Katheline and Jack Leone Collection.*

Rectangular pin cluster of grapes, c. 1870. *Courtesy of the Katheline and Jack Leone Collection.*

"Defend Your Country." Uncle Sam rolling up his sleeves. Enamel. U.S. Army painting. *Courtesy of the Katheline and Jack Leone Collection.*

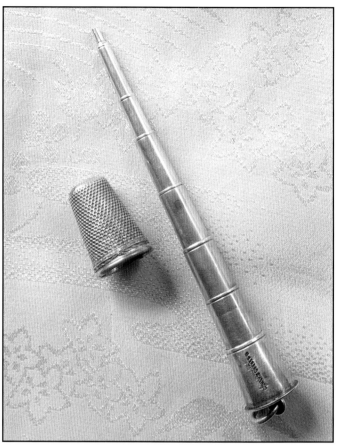

Telescoping, figural pencil. *Courtesy of the Katheline and Jack Leone Collection.*

Figural stamp box, circa 1890. Worn mark, possibly Gorham. *Courtesy of the Katheline and Jack Leone Collection.*

Patriotic pin. Copper shield shaped, possibly World War I. No prices this page. *Courtesy of the Katheline and Jack Leone Collection.*

Gold enamel. *Courtesy of the Katheline and Jack Leone Collection.*

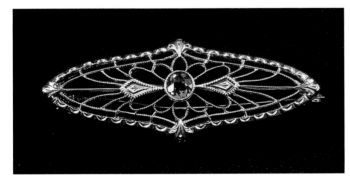

Lace pin. *Courtesy of the Katheline and Jack Leone Collection.*

Gold and pearls. *Courtesy of the Katheline and Jack Leone Collection.*

Gold brooch. *Courtesy of the Katheline and Jack Leone Collection.*

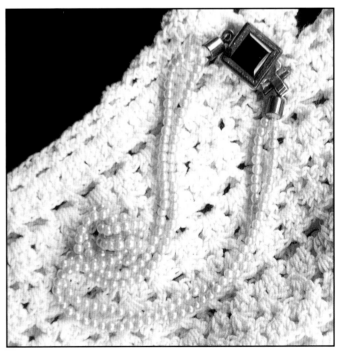

Seed pearl bracelet. *Courtesy of the Katheline and Jack Leone Collection.*

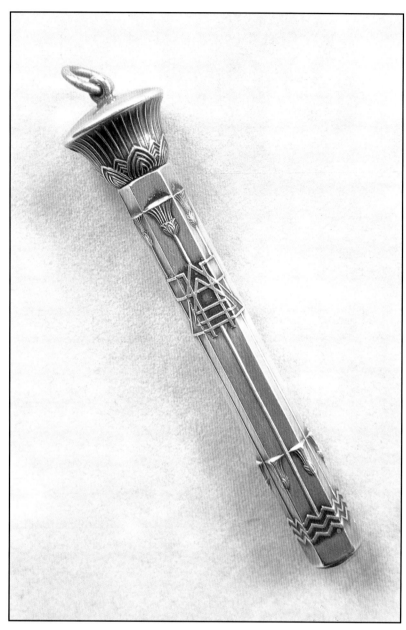

Sterling Silver pencil, marked Fairchild. No prices this page. *Courtesy of the Katheline and Jack Leone Collection.*

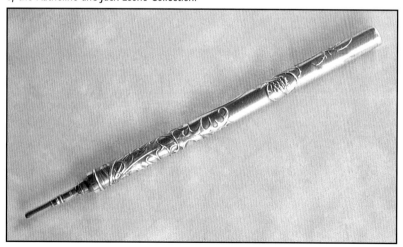

Silver pencil. *Courtesy of the Katheline and Jack Leone Collection.*

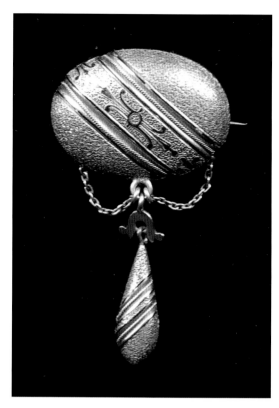

Chatelane watch pin. *Courtesy of the Katheline and Jack Leone Collection.*

Reverse of locket. *Courtesy of the Katheline and Jack Leone Collection.*

Another area that may interest beginning collectors, an area in which one can still find bargains, is metal jewelry boxes. Three metal jewelry caskets, cast of white metal and patinated to appear to be made of bronze. $25-$55.

Two jewelry boxes. $25-$55 each.

Small jewelry box, souvenir of Grant's Tomb, circa 1900. $25-$35.

Unusual jewelry casket in the Art Nouveau style. $55-$75.

Advertising jewelry box, embossed "Limay Bros. Jewelers." $25-$35.

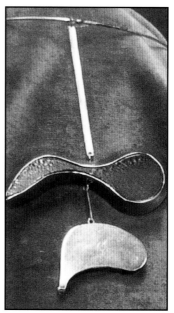

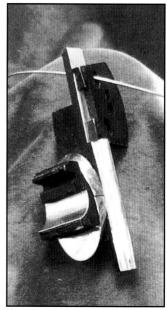

Photographs of jewelry owned by Louise Nevelson. Photo copyright Kathleen Keating, 2003. When I researched the auction of Louise Nevelson's property, I discovered that her son had decided to sell some of her belongings. Nevelson had died in 1989, and her son inherited some of her property. Unfortunately, I missed the opportunity to personally photograph some of her jewelry, but was able to obtain permission to include these photos in this book. Nevelson was a dramatic woman, and often wore outrageous jewelry and clothing (she was known to pin fabrics together to create her own outfits. Indeed, several of the lacquer boxes were filled with safety pins!)

Music/jewelry box, souvenir of Munich. $45-$65.

Top of a Japanese lacquer box owned by Louise Nevelson, American sculptor, 1904-1988. Inside are pieces of mirrors used by Nevelson in her sculptures. When you have the opportunity to get to a flea market early some Sunday morning, you may discover wonderful things. Here is an example of the kind of serendipitous find I'm describing: an entire lot of Japanese and Chinese lacquer boxes that were once owned by the sculptor Louise Nevelson were laid out on a blanket one steamy July morning, for sale at a few dollars apiece. The vendor had bought a box-lot at an auction and had made back his purchase price plus a profit on one or two items, and was offering the remainder at a very low price.

Another Japanese lacquer trinket box owned by Louise Nelson.

Jewelry box, "C. B. Karlen, White Plains, NY" circa 1920. Original boxes help to locate information about jewelers.

Cardboard box, "J. E. Griffith, Jeweler and Silversmith, Hartford, Connecticut."

Plastic ring box, circa 1950.

Trinket box covered with charms from Cracker Jack boxes, circa 1940.

Flower. N.P. *Courtesy of the Katheline and Jack Leone Collection.*

Pocket knife with blade, scissors, and file. French punch mark. N.P. *Courtesy of the Katheline and Jack Leone Collection.*

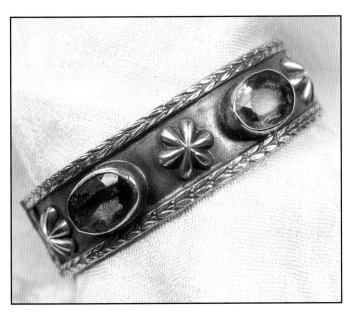

Cuff bracelet. From Panama.

Reverse of previous image.

Flower with moonstones prong set, topaz center. 1920s-30s,

Aluminum Jewelry

*I*n 1874, it was written that "Although so abundant, it is only within a few years that the metal has appeared in a free state, and even at the present time the manufacture is too expensive to admit of its common use in the arts ... the difficulty encountered in soldering and welding aluminum and the high cost of its production, have seriously interfered with its extensive application in the arts. It can hardly be said to have fulfilled all the expectations that were raised at the time of the revival of its manufacture introduced in 1855 by Deville." (Ripley, pp. 367-368, volume 1.) By 1894, however, *The Youth's Companion* offered a selection of items to be sent to the new subscriber as a gift (with the value of $1.00) and one of those premiums was an aluminum hair ornament. In twenty years time, aluminum went from being valued as a precious, rare metal to being offered as a free give-away along with a magazine subscription.

Aluminum, in its metallic form, is not found in nature, although it is one of the most common metals on earth. At the time it was isolated and produced in small metallic grains by Wöhler in 1845, and in larger quantities by Deville in 1855, there was a belief that an inevitable alliance between man and nature could lead to the production of aluminum on a larger scale, that the small amounts of metal were only a hint of the possibilities that were to follow. (Nichols, pp. 59-68.)

The shift in the relative value of aluminum between 1874 and 1894 reflects the vast changes that occurred with the discovery in the 1870s that the large quantities of the oxide alumina (of which aluminum is created) existed in bauxite and could be refined from bauxite into the metallic form, but primarily with the discovery in 1886 of the electrolytic process of manufacturing aluminum.

With the electrolytic process, discovered independently by the Hall (American) and Héroult (French), limitless quantities of aluminum could be produced, economically. The price of aluminum fell from about $12 a pound in the mid-1880s to under a dollar a pound by the early 1890s and below fifty cents by the end of the nineteenth century. But it was still the most modern metal, fresh, different, new. It was considered novel, and in the age of novelty, this was significant. Aluminum was put to use replacing other metals. But also, new uses were created for the innovative metal. It was not only light, about one quarter the weight of silver, but ductile and malleable. While it is similar in its whiteness to sterling silver, it doesn't oxidize.

Ideas for the possible uses of aluminum proliferated. At the very top of the Washington Monument is an 8.8-inch high pyramid made of aluminum, which was cast by a young man from Philadelphia named William Frishmuth. Frishmuth's aluminum casting was so rare in 1884 that it was put on display in Tiffany's in New York City prior to being set into the Washington Monument. A baby rattle (1856) was made of aluminum and gold, diamonds, emeralds, and coral for the Prince Imperial; and an aluminum and gilded bronze centerpiece was made by Charles Christofle in 1858 for Napoleon III. (Nichols, p. 192).

Among the earliest suggestions for the use of aluminum was jewelry, yet early aluminum jewelry is rare today. It's sometimes set with semi-precious or precious stones, is often combined with gold, and is extremely difficult to find.

By 1874, various alloys of aluminum were used. "An alloy of aluminum with silver, called third silver (tiers-argent), composed of one third silver and two thirds aluminum, is chiefly employed for forks, spoons, and tea service, and is harder than silver and is more easily engraved ... Mixed with copper in the proportion of 10 parts aluminum and 90 of copper, it forms a beautiful aluminum bronze, now frequently employed for the manufacture of watch cases, watch chains, imitation jewelry ..." Aluminum and aluminum and celluloid hair ornaments were advertised in *Youth's Home Companion* as early as 1890, and they were also shown as accessories in *Vogue* magazine, 1914 (Mulvagh, p. 34).

Collecting aluminum jewelry offers an interesting challenge. Because so little has been written about it, it's difficult to know exactly what might be found. Relatively old pieces, certainly of late nineteenth century, early twentieth century vintage, can still be found at fairly low prices, although very early pieces (prior to 1885) are difficult to find. Early aluminum jewelry, mixed with gold and/or precious stones is almost never found outside museum collections.

Recommended Reading

Bonita J. Campbell, Wendell August Forge, *Seventy Five Years of Artistry in Metal*.
Sarah Nicols, *Aluminum By Design*.

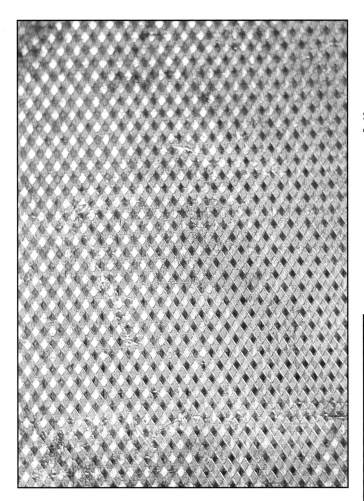

Sheet of textured aluminum, circa 1890.

Very early aluminum brooch on original card. Extremely rare. N.P.

Hand painted glass photograph of the Washington Monument and the Capitol Building in an aluminum frame. Circa 1890. At the very tip of the Washington monument was a pyramid cast of aluminum, placed there in 1884.

Pocket watch, engine turned case. Circa 1890. $350-$450.

Back of watch case, with watch key.

Interior, marked "Warranted Aluminum."

Aluminum and celluloid hair comb, circa 1890. This piece was die-stamped and riveted to the celluloid comb, 5 1/2" x 2". $125-$150.

Ad from 1890s *Youth's Home Companion* for an aluminum hair comb.

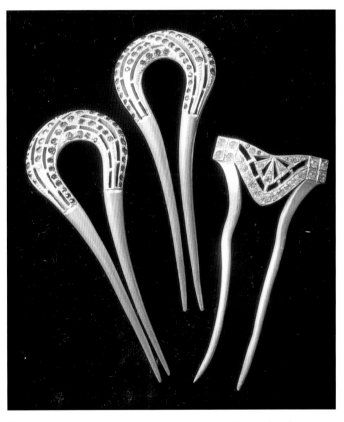

Aluminum and rhinestone comb.

Aluminum hair ornament with celluloid comb. Set with more than one hundred small stones that make it glisten. Circa 1910, 5". $125-$150.

Art deco style hair combs made of aluminum, with simulated prong settings for the pastes. Circa 1920, 4 1/4" x 1 1/2". $75-$125 pair.

Pair of aluminum hair ornaments, circa 1910. Hand engraved, set with rhinestones. $75-$125 pair.

Ribbon worn by the "Standard Bearer" in a July 4 parade, circa 1900. $55-$65.

Aluminum jewelry box, circa 1910. $35-$45.

Cover of photo album, pressed aluminum cards and flowers. Circa 1890.

Aluminum calling card case. $35-$55.

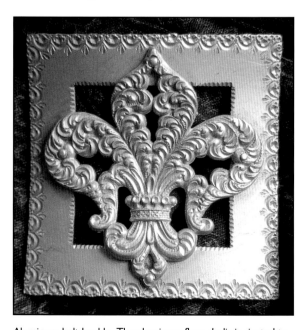

Aluminum belt buckle. The aluminum fleur-de-lis is riveted to the base with tiny aluminum pins. Circa 1890, 2 1/2" x 2 1/2". $125-$150.

Die stamped aluminum collapsible cup, with soccer players. Circa 1920, $75-$95. *Courtesy Edward Heller.*

Aluminum and celluloid barrette with pastes (some missing stones), textured surface hand cut to reveal smoother, shinier surfaces. Circa 1890, 4 1/4" x 1". $50-$75. Aluminum and nickel silver barrette with simulated prong setting for the pastes. Circa 1900, 2" x 3". $50-$75.

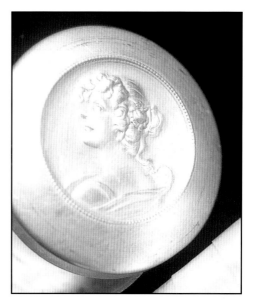

Aluminum collapsible cup, with die stamped bust of a woman. Circa 1920, $75-$95.

Pierced design aluminum pin, circa 1910. $25-$35.

Aluminum collapsible cup, with die stamped bust of an Egyptian style woman. Circa 1920, $75-$95.

Aluminum cuff, in the Native American style with hammered stamps and repoussé design. Circa 1940 (1 1/2" x 6 1/2") asymmetrical, interesting design. Extremely rare. N.P.

Aluminum cuff, in the Native American style with hammered stamps and repoussé design with rooster. Unusual piece, highly original. Circa 1940 (2 1/4" x 6 1/2"). Extremely rare. N.P.

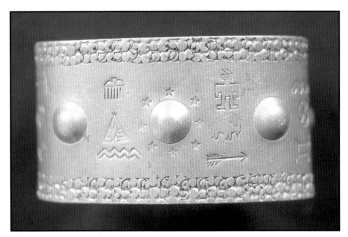

Aluminum cuff, in the Native American style with hammered stamps and repoussé design. Not as well crafted as the previous two bracelets, but like silver bracelets of the same genre. Circa 1940, $75-$100.

Two aluminum bracelets in the Native American style, circa 1930. Both are handmade and stamped with patterns used by American Indians in the Southwest. $175-$250. The larger bracelet, which is 1 1/4" wide, has repoussè work.

Handmade aluminum pendant on an aluminum chain, circa 1950. $75-$95.

Aluminum bracelet with embossed design of an American Indian in a headdress, a teepee, bow, arrow and hatchet. Circa 1950, $75-$95.

Three piece gorget, circa 1950. In the eighteenth century, gorgets were made of silver and traded by early Americans to Native Americans for furs, and were also given as emblems of peace treaties (see Newman, *Illustrated Dictionary of Silverware*, pp. 154-155, 176-177). $75-$125.

Pendant with geometric Native American design. Chain (18"), pendant (2 1/2"). Circa 1950, $45-$55.

Bracelet with Native American motif, 1 1/2" x 7", $50-$75.

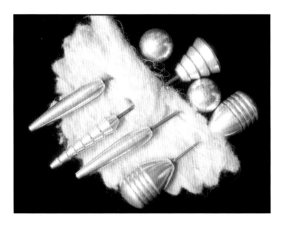

Hat pins on original felt, circ 1940. Set, $200-$235.

Modernistic necklace and bracelet, circa 1950. $155-$175.

Hat pins, circa 1930. One end unscrews so the pin can be threaded through a hat or lapel of a coarse, open fabric. Very Deco, approximately 2 1/4" x 1/2". $35-$60 each.

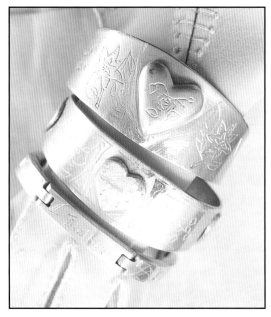

Handmade bracelets. Two with hearts (the inscriptions have been filed off. It's hard not to associate them with a "Dear John" letter. The bottom bracelet is magnificently machined but naively inscribed "Mother," with flowers. Trench art, $50-$75.

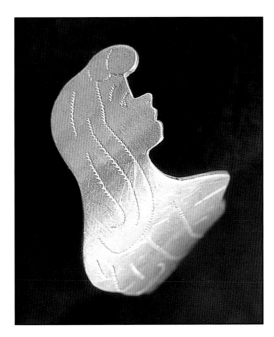

Handmade cuff bracelet, in the shape of a shapely young woman with platform shoes and an upturned nose. Trench art, most likely one of a kind. Made during WWII, approximately 1 1/2" x 6 1/2". $75-$125.

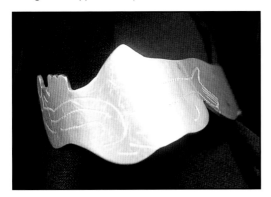

Another view of the cuff bracelet.

Handmade bracelet made from a Japanese Zero shot down in Leyte, 1944 (inscription inside bracelet, half of which has original black paint). Riveted appliqué of cut out shapes, heart, and flowers, one that spins like a propeller. Trench art, probably one of a kind, 2 1/2" x 1 1/4". $150-$175.

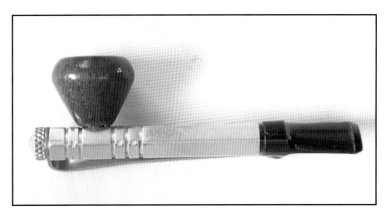

Tie clip with aluminum and wood pipe. "Ceci n'est pas une pipe." (homage to Magritte). Circa 1940, approximately 2 1/2" x 1", $25-$45.

Art deco style belt made of aluminum die stamped with stylized animal with foliate pattern. Circa 1940, 30" x 1 1/2". $65-$85.

Repoussé aluminum belt ornament with links. Circa 1950, 10" x 2". $40-$50. Bracelets, circa 1950, approximately 1 1/4" x 6 1/2". $35-$55.

Two bracelets. $35-$55 each.

Aluminum belt.

Earrings. $35-$55.

Bracelet, approximately 1 1/4" x 6 1/2". $35-$55.

Pendant, dogwood pattern. 19" chain, 2 1/4" pendant, circa 1950. $25-$35.

Aluminum chain, 24", circa 1950. $25-$35.

Necklace.

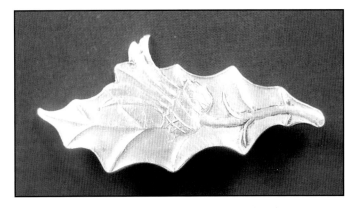

Thistle brooch, August Wendell Forge, circa 1950. $65-$75.

August Wendell Forge, Inc., number 105, pin with sail boat motif. Circa 1950, 2" round. $75-$95.

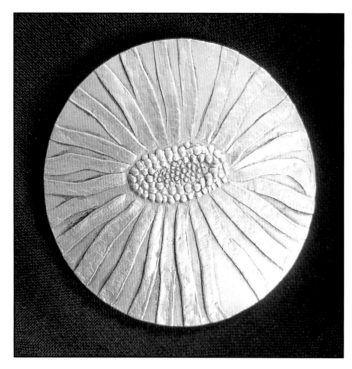

August Wendell Forge, Inc., number 105, pin with daisy motif. Circa 1950, 2" round. $75-$95.

August Wendell Forge, Inc., number 101, rectangular pin with floral motif. Circa 1950, 2 1/2" x 1 1/4". $75-$95.

Reverse of rectangular pin.

Unmarked round pin with golf bag and golf clubs, circa 1950. $65-$75.

August Wendell Forge, Inc., number 100, pendant and bracelet with dressage theme. Circa 1950, $200-$250.

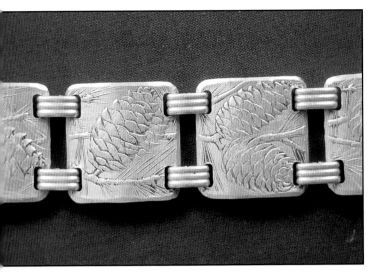

August Wendell Forge, Inc., number 100, bracelet with pine cones and pine needles. Circa 1950, 1 1/4" x 7". $75-$95.

Cape Cod aluminum souvenir bracelet. c. 1950. $35-$55.

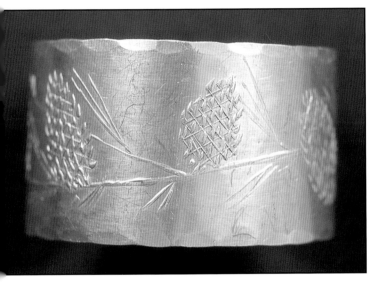

"DePonceau, Chautaugua," cuff bracelet. DePonceau worked for August Wendell Forge until he started his own business in western New York State. $75-$125.

Aluminum and red plastic ring. $175-$225.

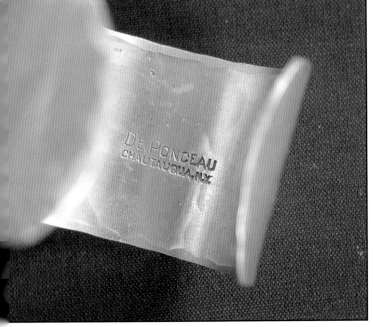

Interior of cuff bracelet, with maker's mark.

Vulcanite

Ebonite, Hard Rubber (Gutta-percha and Other Black Materials)

*A*lthough both hard rubber and gutta-percha had been discovered prior to the nineteenth century, it wasn't until the middle of that century that inventors learned how to make these materials stable enough to be used for production. And both materials offered endless possibilities, from shoes to pontoon boats to breast pumps to napkin rings, from toys to dentures, tents to watch chains, knapsacks to lockets. The range was wide; leave it to the Victorian to find countless possibilities, endless variations, and limitless uses for a new material. Again, although this a material we now take for granted, finding early Vulcanite jewelry can be a challenge. The prices have gone up considerably in the past few years, and one can expect to see lockets in the $250 range and bracelets from $200-$300.

Hard rubber, also called Vulcanite, Ebonite, India-rubber, imitation horn, caoutchouc ivory … and often mistakenly described today as gutta-percha, is the result of the gum product of a cahuchu tree being combined with sulphur at high temperatures (vulcanizing process). This process enabled manufacturers to use the material in a variety of ways, especially as it allowed the material to be exposed to heat without melting and to cold without becoming brittle.

Hard rubber can be discerned from gutta-percha, which looks very much like hard rubber, by rubbing the material with a thumb or finger. If the heat from the minor friction releases a sulphurish or rubbery scent, it's hard rubber. If not, it's gutta-percha. "The absence of the rubbery smell due to the reduction or elimination of sulphur in the vulcanization process is evident on surviving gutta-percha artifacts of today." (Woshner, p.66.)

Hard rubber was molded into many forms. One of the forms we find it in most commonly today is the barrels of nineteenth century fountain pens. But it was also used for flexible bracelets, lockets, watch chains, brooches, fobs, etc. Examples here show Vulcanite as used in pen barrels, cases for mechanical pencils, ink bottles, and a perfume atomizer in the shape of a watch case, patented in 1899 by the American Hard Rubber Company.

Gutta-percha also is made from the sap of a tree, but from a different kind of tree than those that produce the latex used in making hard rubber. Gutta-percha is produced from Malaysian gum trees, and the sap can be formed into objects and retain the shape, without the molding process required for hard rubber. However, unless gutta-percha is subjected to a vulcanization process similar to the one used for Ebonite, the object will disintegrate after a brief period of time. Gutta-percha was used for many of the same types of objects as Vulcanite, but it is far less common to find jewelry made of it than of hard rubber. The one example that I was able to locate is a match safe, molded with a basket-weave pattern. The distinct odor of sulphur emanated from every piece of jewelry that I tested.

Various composition materials were also used in the nineteenth century.

When shopping for jewelry made of Vulcanite, be prepared to hear some interesting comments about the material itself. One person described it as, "a substance much like papier-mâché." Another said that the more sulphur that was in it, the harder it would be.

Recommended Reading

Charles Slack, *Noble Obsession: Charles Goodyear, Thomas Hancock, and the Race to Unlock the Greatest Industrial Secret of the Nineteenth Century.*

Mike Woshner, *India-Rubber and Gutta-Percha in the Civil War Era.*

Ebonite necklace with the profile of Dionysus on the 2" pendant. Circa 1860, $150-$175.

Book entitled *The Romance of Rubber*, circa 1900. Black hard rubber is also called Vulcanite and Ebonite. It is not gutta-percha, although it is often labeled as such at antiques shows and flea markets.

44" ebonite chain, with round links. $75-$125.

Unusual Vulcanite necklace with jet flower, metal tassels, Vulcanite cross. 16" chain, 6" pendant and cross, circa 1860, $350-$425.

Ebonite chains came in a wide variety of styles. $75-$125.

Smooth vulcanite locket with floral designs in the interior. Original glass and bezel. Circa 1870, 2" x 1 1/2". $45-$65.

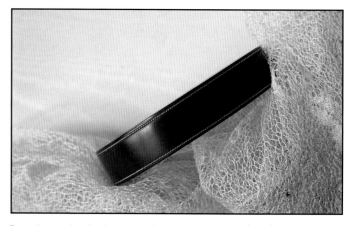

Bracelet of vulcanite and gold. This bracelet and the next one were probably both parts of sets of two identical bracelets that would have been worn one on each wrist. $50-$75.

Vulcanite watch chain with flat oval links, 12". Circa 1860, $65-$85.

Bracelet made of vulcanite and twisted gold wire. $50-$75.

Long watch chain with nearly round links (18") with brooch (2" x 2"), textured and smooth vulcanite with simulated screws that appear to be holding a raised plaque that says "Souvenir." Circa 1860. $125-$175.

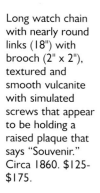

Tortoise shell with pique (gold) slide pencil, circa 1840. $350-$425. The gold wires inlaid into the black hard rubber of the bracelets above emulate the pique work in this tortoise shell pencil.

Bracelet made of ebonite and gold with severe but elegant lines. $250-$325.

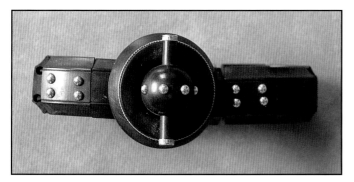

Top view of bracelet.

Bracelet with padlock, molded black hard rubber segments and composition. Approximately 1" x 7". $250-$325.

Vulcanite cuff bracelet with flowers. $200-$250.

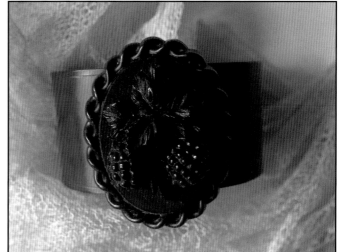

Black hard rubber cuff bracelet with raspberries. Approximately 2 1/4" x 6". $250-$325.

Ebonite bracelet, with swivel to adjust size. Black glass beads at terminals, with overhand knot. $225-$250.

Pressed horn and gold pique brooch, circa 1860. Many materials were used to emulate tortoiseshell or Whitby jet, including molded horn. $125-$150.

Vulcanite watch chain with black lacquered findings. Circa 1870. $75-$95.

Vulcanite brooch in the shape of a miner's pick. Circa 1860, $125-$150.

Brooch, cluster of grapes surrounded by a rustic, woven twig motif. Made of jet, circa 1850, 2 1/2" x 2 1/4". $275-$325.

Mourning ring. 14 kt. gold, black onyx, white enamel with gold dots, gold trellis-work, and seed pearl. Circa 1870, $150-$175. Much of the black jewelry shown here was worn in mourning.

Ebonite bar pin with crescent moon and orbs. 2 1/4" x 1/2". $75-$95.

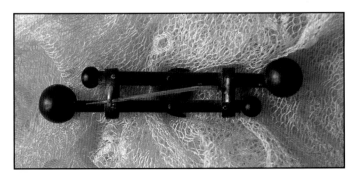

Back of ebonite bar pin, showing tube hinge.

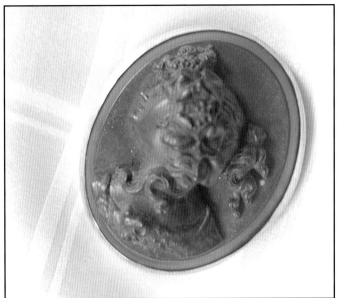

Brooch/pendant made of vulcanite, with gold bezel. 2" x 1 1/2". $250-$325.

Pansy brooch, vulcanite. 2" x 1 1/2", $50-$75. Pansies were used to symbolize remembrance.

Composition brooch with hand holding a basket of cherries. Intricately molded, details include a lace sleeve and miniature bracelet on the wrist holding the woven basket. 2 1/2" x 1 1/4". $225-$250.

177

Elegantly molded hand holding wreath, made of composition. 2 1/2" x 1 1/4". $225-$250.

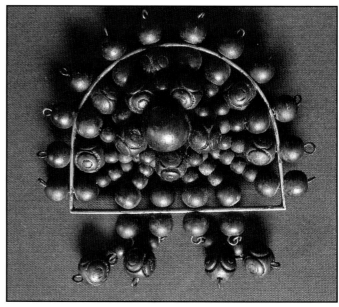

Black and red hard rubber beads and silver flat wire brooch, 2 1/2" x 3 1/2". $75-$125.

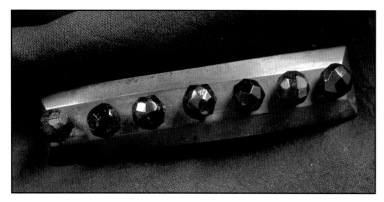

Simple vulcanite bar pin with black glass beads, 3 1/2" x 3/4", $50-$75.

Brooch made of vulcanite and gold. Unusual shape, with a top half-round shape arching over a ball and teardrop-shaped pendants. Circa 1870. $125-$150.

Vulcanite brooch with a cluster of grapes. Circa 1865, $125-$150.

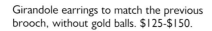

Girandole earrings to match the previous brooch, without gold balls. $125-$150.

Delicate vulcanite earrings with original gold wires. 3/4" x 1/4", $75-$95.

Hair ornament made of vulcanite, with pierced clover design. 7" x 1 1/4", $75-$95.

Other nineteenth century objects made of vulcanite, ebonite or hard rubber are an inkwell, atomizer in the shape of a watch case, patented by the American Hard Rubber Company in 1899, and a pencil. The match safe (rectangular box with basket weave) seems to be made of gutta-percha. $75-$250.

Miniature pipe in the shape of a woman's leg, with high heeled boot and garter. 3 1/2" x 3/4", $125-$150.

Match safe commemorating King Edward, circa 1901. Mint condition (black hard rubber with no oxidation or scratches), 2" x 1 1/2", $125-$150.

Aigrette made of bezel set cut black glass, circa 1880. 4 1/2" x 2 1/2", $75-$100.

Tiny black metal brooch with crescent and pansy, circa 1860. $35-$45.

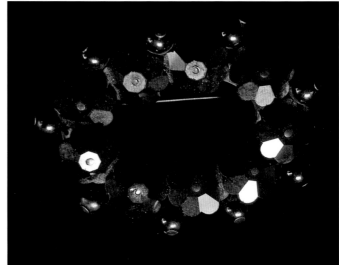

Oval brooch made of faceted black glass flowers and round beads, mid-twentieth century, clearly influenced by nineteenth century jewelry. 2" x 1 1/2", $50-$75.

Pens with barrels made of hard rubber: "Waterman's" Ripple 55 (red and black. Hard rubber could be made in colors other than black), 5 1/2", with gold-filled trim ($125); "Waterman's" 0314, early (circa 1890) eye dropper fill with gold-filled, repoussè overlay, 5 1/2"; "Mead Fountain Pen Co." engraved silver overlay 5 1/4"; "Waterman's" 412 1/2 VS, 3 1/2" (vest pocket safety with silver overlay), circa 1900; "Waterman's" 412 1/2 (silver overlay), circa 1890, 4 3/4"; "Waterman's" 16 POC with gold-filled trim, circa 1920. $175-$600.

Pencil cases (the exterior of a nineteenth century pencil was called the "case." The mechanism and trim may be made of other materials.) made of ebonite: unmarked, 3 1/4", engine turned hard rubber and gold filled trim; engine turned ebonite, "A. G. Day's" (Austin Goodyear Day, not the Horace Day who Charles Goodyear had the patent infringement lawsuit against) Patent, August 10, 1858; smooth hard rubber, no maker's mark, patent October 17, 1871; pen/pencil marked "Mabie, Todd & Co." #4, engine turned; Goodyear's Patent May 6, 1851; smooth hard rubber with slide mechanism, date unclear, Goodyear Patent; red rubber, engine turned, magic pencil patented March 21, 1871. $175-$300.

Celluloid, Bakelite, and Plastic

*C*elluloid is known as the precursor to plastic. It was originally invented to be used as a less expensive substitute for ivory pool balls. By 1883, De Puy describes the usages of celluloid to include "billiard balls are made of C at half the price of ivory, and are said to be equally elastic, while more durable ... even a fine toothed comb is 25 per cent. Cheaper than ivory ..., whip, cane, umbrella handles ..., chessmen, and the handles of knives and forks ... The freedom of C. from sulphur, and the natural flesh-color which can be imparted to it, have caused it to be extensively substituted for India rubber in the manufacture of dental blanks, or the gums, and other attachments of artificial teeth."

He goes on to say, "C. can also be mottled so as to imitate the finest tortoise-shell, and its elasticity renders it much less liable to breakage ... Beautiful jewelry is made of it in imitation of the most elaborately carved coral, reproducing all the shades of the genuine article." (De Puy, vol. I, p. 398.) Of course, one of the problems not anticipated in this description is the volatility of celluloid. Using it as material for shirt cuffs and collars could be dangerous, despite the claim that it "can be worn for months without injury." (De Puy, Vol. I, p. 398.)

When consulting this mid-nineteenth century cyclopedia, another interesting description of the benefits of using celluloid (this time in place of porcelain) caught my attention. Remember, this was in the day long before dolls were made out of plastic. In fact, it was long before plastic was even invented (although the material mentioned is certainly a precursor to plastic): "As a substitute for porcelain, C. is used for the heads of dolls, which can be hammered against a hard floor without danger of fracture." (De Puy, vol. I, p. 398.) The "C." mentioned here is celluloid, of course.

Recommended Reading

Tessa Clark, *Bakelite Style.*
Susan Mossman (editor), *Early Plastics, Perspectives 1850-1950.*

Celluloid magic pencil in the shape of a woman's shoe with gold buttons, circa 1890. $350-$475.

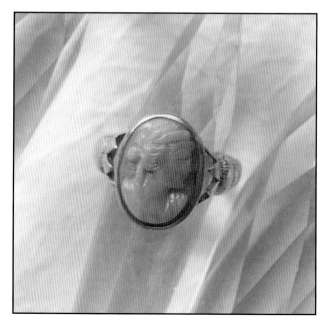

Coral cameo ring, worn. Circa 1880, $125-$150.

Coral beads arranged as bunches of grapes, with gilded leaves and tendrils, earrings and brooch. Circa 1920, $125-$150.

Glass beads, gold filigree, with white dog-toothed shaped beads. Circa 1950. $35-$45.

Festoon necklace of gold-plated metal and coral colored glass beads. Circa 1920, $55-$75 (unsigned).

16" string of branch coral, circa 1920. $75-$125.

Coral colored ladies pens, circa 1920. Gold Bond "Stonite" in tangerine plastic, lever fill, 14k warranted nib, 3 1/2" ($65); orange and white marbleized pen with 14k warranted nib, lever fill, 3 3/4" ($45), red and white marbleized pen, gold filled band, 3 3/4" ($45).

"Peter Pan" fountain pen in amber, brown, and cream marbleized plastic, 14k gold nib, eye dropper fill, 2 1/4" ($125); red and black marbleized "Peter Pan" fountain pen, 14k gold nib, 2 1/4" ($125); "Pony" fountain pen in white with gold filled band, 14 k nib marked "Pony" ($100). Circa 1920.

Ladies pens with appliquéd plastic flowers. 1920s, $125-$150 each.

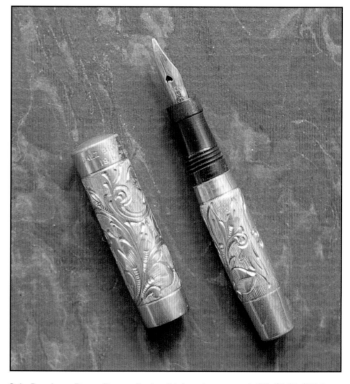

Salz Brothers Peter Pan, rolled gold, hand engraved, 2". $250-$325.

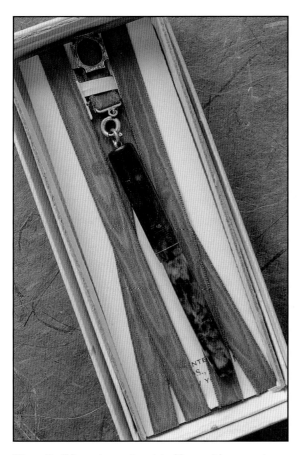

"Peter Pan" fountain pen in original box, with grosgrain ribbon and gold filled slide, 3" ($150).

Range of "Parker" pens and pencils from the 1920s. Beautiful colors, from "Mandarin yellow" to lapis blue. $125-$300.

"Mabie Todd Swan" pens, N/92 (green, yellow, and black) and B/92 (blue, black, and yellow), with gold overfeed nibs, 3 3/4". Circa 1920. $175-$250. "Mabie Todd Swan" fountain pen, also with lever fill, 172/51 (tangerine and black with two gold bands), 4 1/8", circa 1925. $225-$300. "Parker" moiré fountain pens in brown and blue, button fill, circa 1925. $225-$250.

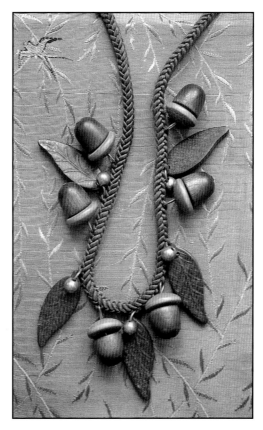

Necklace, silk cord with wooden acorns and leaves. Circa 1930, $75-$125.

Bakelite cherries. *Courtesy Vita Materasso.*

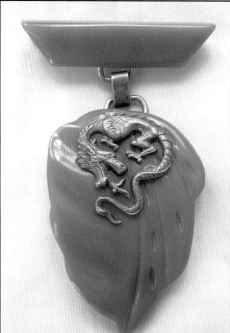

Green and gold bakelite brooch with gilded dragon appliquéd to drop. *Courtesy Vita Materasso.*

White metal brooch. $75-$85. *Courtesy Vita Materasso.*

Bakelite cherries. $250-$350. *Courtesy Vita Materasso.*

Green and gold colored bakelite necklace with filigree spacers. *Courtesy Vita Materasso.*

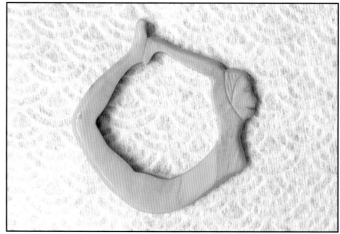

Bracelet in the shape of a very flexible woman. N.P. *Courtesy Vita Materasso.*

Bakelite hat brooch, circa 1950. N.P. *Courtesy Chris Petrillo.*

Bird, clear plastic with brown plastic wing, 2" x 4". $65-$85.

This cheerful, colorful dress clip attracted my attention many years ago. It is unmarked, but may be attributed to Miriam Haskell (see Gordon and Pamfiloff, page75.) N.P.

Cowboy made of plastic with a leather lasso. Circa 1950, 2" x 1 1/2". $65-$75.

Dress clip, orange and green. N.P.

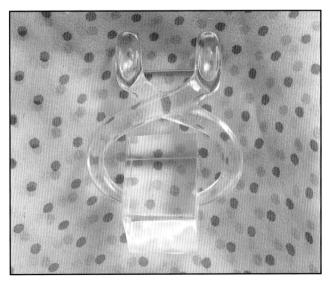

Clear plastic ice tongs, with block of plastic ice that swivels. $65-$85.

Multicolored beads, 24". $45-$65.

Textured, clustered yellow plastic beads with green leaves. 14". $75-$125.

Mother-of-Pearl

*I*t was not unusual to find several mother-of-pearl pins with words or initials made of wire on them at a flea market a few years ago. As a matter of fact, they were so common that most people passed them over. I bought a few to use as examples, but when we were visiting the Wadsworth Atheneum recently and saw a Calder wire sculpture in which he had twisted the wire to form someone's name, I decided that it would be interesting to find more early examples of wire and mother-of-pearl jewelry. It may well be that it was common enough in the late 1880s and early 1900s to see such jewelry, and perhaps Calder was even inspired by it. Certainly ads from *Youth's Companion* encouraged young people to learn how to craft such jewelry (and a kit could be ordered to accommodate an interest in making wire jewelry at home, with "no noise, no dust nor dirt." *Youth's Companion*, October 25, 1894, p. 503).

But a recent expedition to the flea markets, perusing the wares of over 500 dealers brought forth not even one wire and mother-of-pearl brooch. This is what happens with antique jewelry: objects appear to be fairly common at a certain stage and because of this, very few people buy them. Gradually, however, these items become more and more scarce and not only does it become more difficult to find them, but the prices make it difficult to afford them! For those of us who've been around antiques for a long time, it's hard to adjust to something that used to cost fifty cents now costing fifty dollars.

Name pins, wire (some on mother-of-pearl shapes) 1890-1940, $25-$65.

Brooch, nineteenth century scene painted on mother-of-pearl, with a celluloid border. $75-$95.

Aide memoire, made of ivory with inscribed with a gorilla, circa 1870s. *Courtesy of Rachel Marks Antiques.*

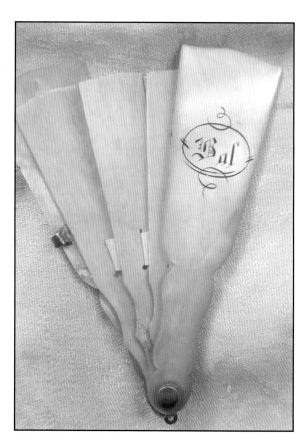

Bal de carnet made of mother-of-pearl, in the shape of a fan. Circa 1870, $175-$250.

Three mid-nineteenth century aide memoires made of ivory, one with silver pique inlay. $175-$250.

Mechanical pencils made with gold and mother-of-pearl, circa 1870. $225-$275. Propelling pencils: slabs of abalone, rolled gold, patented December 5, 1871; mother-of-pearl slabs alternated with engraved rolled gold, patented May 14, 1872; corrugated mother-of-pearl with rolled gold trim, unmarked, circa 1872.

Aide memoire, made of mother-of-pearl with silver inlay. Circa 1870, $225-$300.

Carving in deep relief, mother-of-pearl aide memoire, circa 1860. $350-$425.

Small brooches with square wire formed into an initial or name ("Mother"), circa 1900, $55-$75.

Aide memoire made of composition with mother-of-pearl inlay. Circa 1850 (dated), $250-$325.

Tortoise shell aide memoire. *Courtesy of Adele Golden of the Garden Gate Antiques.* $350-$425.

These beautiful examples of aide memoires are the predecessors of Palm Pilots. *Courtesy of Rachel Marks Antiques.*

Sterling silver aide memoire. $300-$500 each. *Courtesy of Rachel Marks Antiques.*

Gun metal and gold with three opals, aide memoire. Circa 1910, $225-$250.

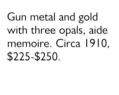

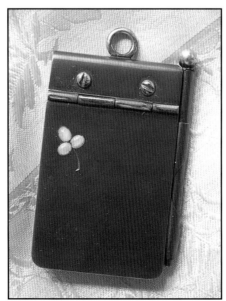

Aide memoire with dragons. *Courtesy of private collection.*

Scheibler aide memoire. $500-$700. *Courtesy of Rachel Marks Antiques.*

Examples of the Aesthetic style. $500-$700. *Courtesy of Rachel Marks Antiques.*

Courtesy of Adele Golden of the Garden Gate Antiques. $275-$325.

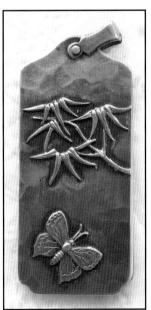

$500-$700. *Courtesy of Rachel Marks Antiques.*

Reverse of previous aide memoire.

Hair Work

*W*hat could be more democratic than jewelry made of the hair of friends and family members? Hair jewelry is really fascinating, once you get past the "ewww" factor (as in "ewww, what is that?"). Jewelry was made with hair, it was made to hold locks of hair, and it was embellished with hair. This is an absolutely perfect example of something that used to be passed over at flea markets and antiques shows. Until people were willing to understand it better, it was perceived as a bit, well, creepy. But there are some absolutely beautiful examples and hair jewelry is now quite pricey (it is delicate and thus difficult to find in good condition). One example shown here includes a Daguerreotype that is most likely a portrait of the individual whose hair was used to create the bracelet.

Recommended Reading

C. Jeanenne Bell, *Collector's Encyclopedia of Hairwork Jewelry.*

Hair bracelet with tintype under glass. $250-$325. *Courtesy of Giselle De Rienzo Antiques.*

Necklace. $250-$325. *Courtesy of Giselle De Rienzo Antiques.*

Floral ornament made of hair. N.P.

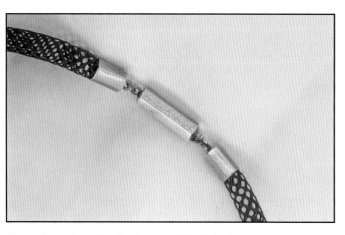

Clasp of necklace (detail). *Courtesy of Giselle De Rienzo Antiques.*

Slogan Buttons, Pin-back Buttons, and Masonic, Etc.

Collecting slogan buttons or pin-back buttons can be an engaging pursuit for someone who's interested in American history. Buttons are sometimes quite striking, usually visually appealing, and often of historic interest. The phrases are enigmatic today, and finding out what they were originally intended to mean is half the fun! One button has an image of a rather sad looking dog, surrounded by the phrase "they gotta quit kickin' my dawg aroun'." This is the lyric of a song, "Firemen's Celebration," written in the mid-1890s and published by the W. F. Miller and Company, 134 Park Row, New York. The song lyrics go like this:
1. Ev'ry time I come to town
The boys keep kickin' my dawg aroun'
Makes no difference if he is a houn'
They gotta quit kickin' my dawg aroun'
2. Me an' Lem Briggs an' old Bill Brown
Took a load of corn to town
My old Jim dawg, ornery old cuss
He just naturally follored us.
3. As we drive past Johnson's store
A passel of yaps come out the door
Jim he scooted behind a box
With all them fellers a-throwin' rocks
4. They tied a can to old Jim's tail
An' run him past the county jail
That just naturally made us sore
Lem, he cussed, and Bill, he swore.
5. Me an' Lem Briggs an' old Bill Brown
Lost no time in a-gitten down
We wiped them fellers on the ground
For kickin' my old dawg, Jim, around.
6. Jim seen his duty there an' then
He lit into them gentlemen
He shore mussed up the courthouse square
With rags an' meat an' hide an' hair.
7. Repeat verse 1

http://www.grandfolkies.com/qsandas.htm

Dennis Morgan was a star for Warner's Brothers and the button was a give-away from Quaker Puffed Wheat and Rice: "shot from guns" circa 1940.

Collecting can be based on a theme. As an example, there are several buttons awarded as prizes for handwriting skills. The Palmer Method Merit button with the blue edge and the hand holding the pen was awarded after the recipient mastered "the first twenty-five drills in the Palmer Method Manual." The gold Palmer Method Merit button, with the laurel, scroll, and quill, was given only after the recipient had mastered the first sixty drills (this particular button was given to Joe Palis). The blue and gold enameled Palmer Method button was made by G. Balfour Company in Attleboro, Massachusetts.

"Ma Winkle" was a cartoon character, and was one of the figures that adorned buttons that were found as premiums in Pep cereal, made by Kellogg's. Kellogg's Pep sponsored a radio show called "The Adventures of Superman" (for an audio clip of the 1945 radio show, go tohttp://www.old-time.com/premiums/radiopremiums12.html).

Masonic emblem with Star of David. Twelve colored stones represent the original tribes of Israel. 1/2 carat mine-cut diamond. $1,950-$2,150. *Courtesy Tom and Mary Valentino of Other's Oldies.*

Sterling silver pendant, 3 1/2" x 2". Hand-engraved with Masonic symbols on one side and the inscription" Terry Radcliffe, Hirams Mark Lodge, No.65, Amenia" [New York] on the other. Circa 1890, $75-$95.

Masonic emblem: "1921 Orient Council R. & S. Masters to P. T. III. Comp. Frank W. Tucker" engraved on the inside, "1963-1964 Orient Council R. & S. Masters to Johannes Vanderhoeff, Jr." 14 kt, total weight of 1/2 carat, 5 diamonds at 10 points each, opal, mother-of-pearl on handle of trowel, in original fitted case. $1,200-$1,400. *Courtesy Tom and Mary Valentino of Other's Oldies.*

Detail of above.

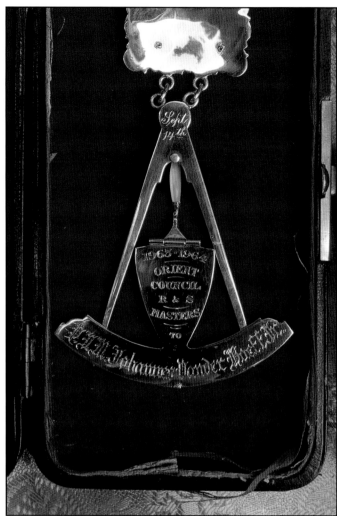

Another detail.

"32nd Degree," double-headed eagle, 2 half carat mine-cut diamonds, 2 rubies, 14 kt. Gold with enamel, watch fob, circa 1920. $2,800-$3,000. *Courtesy Tom and Mary Valentino of Other's Oldies.*

Watch fob shown closed.

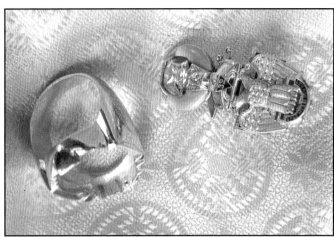

Fraternal organization: ring. *Courtesy Tom and Mary Valentine of Others' Oldies.*

B'nai B'rinth ring, c. 1940. N.P. *Private collection.*

Watch fob shown open with Masonic symbols.

Pins: Cornell University lower right, gold with enamel. $15-$55.

New York State Teachers Association Service pin, gold. $50-$75.

Beat Union. Football rival of Union college. $5-$10.

Red, white, and blue buttons. Union membership and political action committee. $5-$10.

"Friend of Hoffa." $25-$45.

"We Want 10 Cents Per Hour Raise." $5-$8.

"I am a Right-Wing 'Extremist'"

"Don't Blame Me…"

"I Voted Democratic."

"American Women's Voluntary Services;" "National Association of Letter Carriers USA;" "United Office and Professional Workers of America CIO."

Personality and Comic buttons.

Pinbacks: "They Gotta Quit Kickin' My Dawg Aroun,'" "Brought One," "Fireman's Celebration" (W. F. Miller & Co., 134 Park Row, New York, July 21, 1896), "Duffy's dubl-duck" (Union Label, Local 115), 1896-1950, $1-$30.

Handwriting awards. Palmer Method, 1920s-40s. $5-$12.

Who can resist a button when it happens to have your surname emblazoned on it? This button was created for Crosby High School in Connecticut.

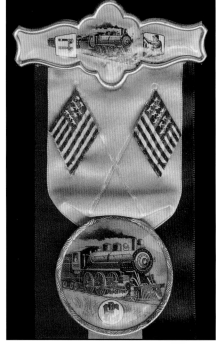

Locomotive.

George Washington. Various buttons and ribbons worn in parades.

Lake Luzerne Lodge.

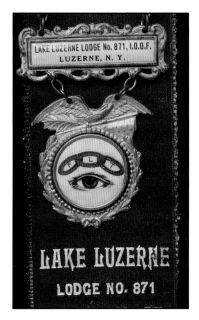

"Chairman: Historic Week Schuylerville, New York, October 13-18, 1912.

Aluminum.

Agate Jewelry

Agate and Carnelian bracelet. *Courtesy of the Gerald Schultz of the Antique Gallery.* $1150-$1250.

Agate bracelets: agate and silver, with heart-shaped lock clasp (and woven hair), $850-$950; four lobed pieces of agate, amethyst and silver with hand-engraved buckle clasp, $1,150-$1,250; crest-shaped agate bracelet with rivets, $750-$850. *Courtesy Gerald Schultz, The Antique Gallery.*

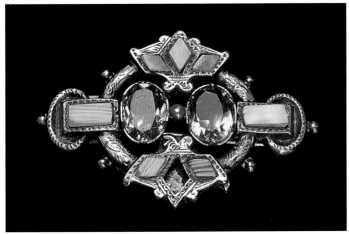

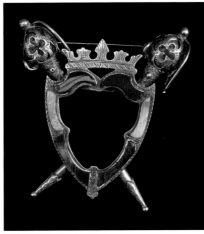

Far left:
Brooch with citrines and agate, unmarked. $275-$350. *Courtesy Gerald Schultz, The Antique Gallery.*

Left:
Agate brooch (locket pin), hallmarked JF, circa 1870. $1,250-$1,350. *Courtesy Gerald Schultz, The Antique Gallery.*

Beads

Silver chain and mounts, sapphire blue glass stones, with artificial pearls. Necklace, circa 1910, $175-$225.

Blue cut glass stones, silver findings, and faux pearls identical to the previous piece, yet with a very different look. Circa 1910, $175-$350. *Courtesy of Ruth Taylor.*

Double strand of graduated simulated pearls in original posh case. Marked "Pearls by André." Circa 1940, 16", $50-$75.

Baroque pearls. $200-$250.

Simulated pearls.

Beads

Festoon necklace from the 1920s, white paté de verre beads with white plastic petals and green enameled metal leaves, on a white enameled 16" chain. $125-$145.

Turquoise pâte de verre beads with filigree mounts on double-link brass chain. Circa 1920, $125-$150.

Amber Bohemian glass and black chain, festoon necklace, circa 1920. $125-$150.

Necklace, with opaque black fluted and round turquoise colored glass beads, 36". $35-$45.

Simulated pearls, circa 1990. $150-175.

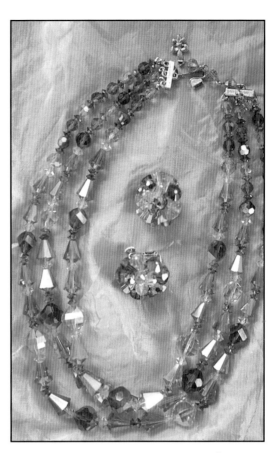

Vêndome beads are top of the line, circa 1950. $175-225.

Kenneth J. Lane Egyptian influence beads. $250-325.

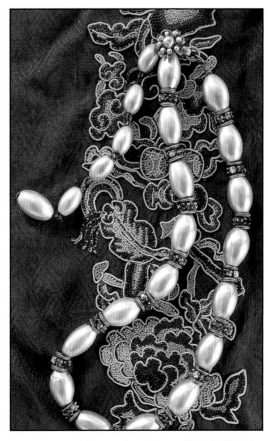

"Miriam Haskell" Simulated pearls, circa 1940. $175-225.

Black and white plastic beaded necklace, circa 1960, 26".
$25-$30.

Earrings with filigree bezels and blue glass stones. $35-$55.

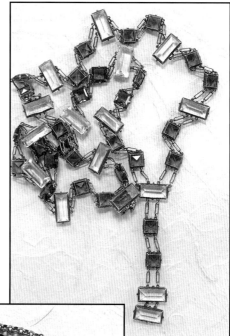

Sautior (30" and 3" pendant) of cut clear and sapphire blue glass, bezel set. $450-$525. *Courtesy of Ruth Taylor.*

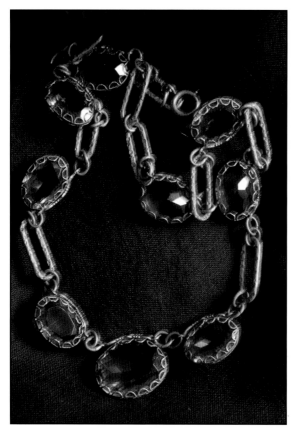

Necklace with oval links, filigree bezels holding blue glass stones, $125-$150.

Necklace with enamel and Czechoslovakian glass, 18" with 2" pendant. $175-$350. *Courtesy of Ruth Taylor.*

Clear and blue Bohemian glass crystal beads on a very fine sterling silver chain. Circa 1910, $125-$150.

Bohemian garnet jewelry, late nineteenth century. Brooches, $200-$1,000. *Courtesy of Ruth Taylor*.

Bohemian garnet necklace, $650-$800. *Courtesy of Ruth Taylor*.

Opaque orange (melon-shaped) and transparent blue glass beads on a fine sterling silver chain. Circa 1910, $125-$150.

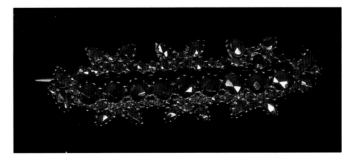

Bohemian garnet brooch. $200-$225.

Men's Jewelry

Sterling silver and gray guilloché cufflinks. $150-$175.

Sterling silver cufflinks with helmet and scroll, made by "Unger Bros.," circa 1900. $285-$325. *Courtesy of Rachel Marks Antiques.*

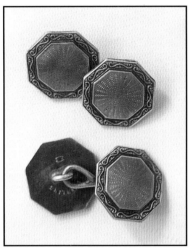

Sterling silver and lavender guilloche cufflinks. $175-$200. *Courtesy of Rachel Marks Antiques.*

Sterling silver cufflinks with a woman in a diaphanous gown. Circa 1890, $175-$200. *Courtesy of Rachel Marks Antiques.*

Silver medallion cufflinks marked "Acme," patented August 24, 1880. $125-$175.

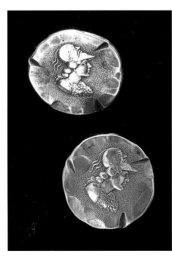

Sterling silver cufflinks with beautifully rendered face of a young woman. $175-$200. *Courtesy of Rachel Marks Antiques.*

Inlaid enamel golfers, cufflinks. *Courtesy of Rachel Marks Antiques.*

Sterling silver stick pin and cufflinks in the original box, marked "Tiffany." Art Nouveau style horse heads. $375-$500.

Sterling silver cufflinks, marked Jensen #30, 1" x 3/4". $350-$400. *Courtesy of Rachel Marks Antiques.*

Faces. Elegant Art Nouveau cufflinks. Rare. N.P. *Courtesy Rachel Marks Antiques.*

Keyhole cufflinks, unmarked, circa 1930. Red and black enamel over gold plated metal. The view through the keyhole shows a couple kissing. $45-$55.

Erotic pencil, unmarked. This gold retractable pencil is embellished with face of a woman in what appears to be an ecstatic state. Circa 1910, $300-$375.

Mesh watch chain with seal and clip, circa 1890. N.P. *Courtesy Thomas Y. Hobart, Jr.*

Watch fob with four medallions, 5 1/2". $250-$325. *Courtesy of Rachel Marks Antiques.*

Nineteenth century watch chain with fraternal insignia on fob. Rolled gold and enamel. N.P. *Courtesy Thomas Y. Hobart, Jr.*

Late nineteenth century watch chain with Etruscan Revival fob. N.P. *Courtesy Thomas Y. Hobart, Jr.*

Money clip. Signed Tiffany, 14kt. gold. Retractable pencil. $400-$425.

Pencils

Magic pencil made by "Fairchild," gold with silver appliqué anchor. Circa 1880, 3 1/2" open. $225-$325. French hallmarked pencil with gold and hand painted enamel work of a winged Cupid in a cage. Circa 1870, 1 3/4" closed. $350-$425.

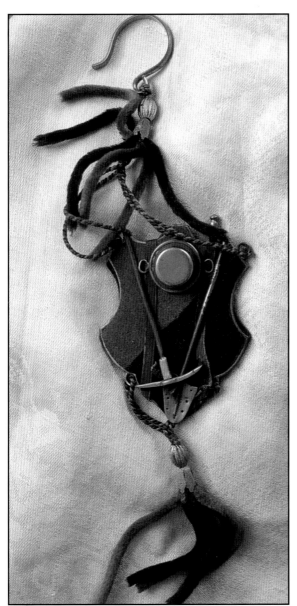

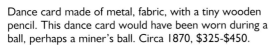

Dance card made of metal, fabric, with a tiny wooden pencil. This dance card would have been worn during a ball, perhaps a miner's ball. Circa 1870, $325-$450.

Sterling silver owl magic pencil, pink cabochon stone eyes, marked with Edward Todd logo. Circa 1870, 1 1/4" closed. $625-$750. On an English hallmarked watch chain, 17".

Sterling silver magic pencil in the shape of a horse head, with pink cabochon stone eyes, marked "Edward Todd." Circa 1880, 1 1/2" closed. $750-$925. On a silver book chain, 17 1/4". $225-$250.

Guilloche red enamel over gold, in the shape of a heart (1"), pierced by a tiny golden pencil in the form of an arrow.$750-$950.

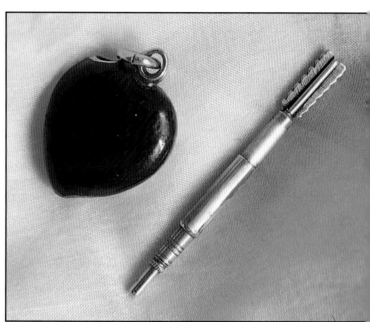

The same enameled heart, with the pencil removed.

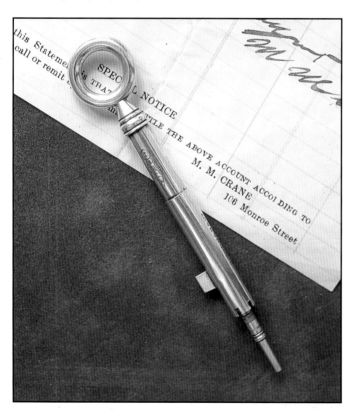

Sterling silver magic pencil in the shape of a Bramah key, made by "Sampson Mordan Company," circa 1880. $925-$1,200.

Vest pocket pencil with race horses, made by "Battin" of Newark, N. J. Circa 1910, sterling silver. $225-$300.

Figural magic pencil in the shape of a baby in a woven basket, sterling silver and silver wash over bronze, circa 1870, unsigned. 2 1/4" open, 1" closed. $750-$825.

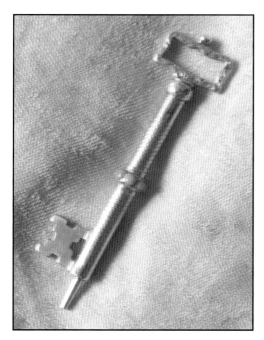

Gold figural pencil in the shape of a key, with cabochon turquoise stones on slider. Registration mark (illegible). $650-$725.

White metal pencil in the shape of King Edward, circa 1905, with Stanhope views by McKee, Dublin, of "A Memory of Stonehaven." No maker's mark. $750-$900.

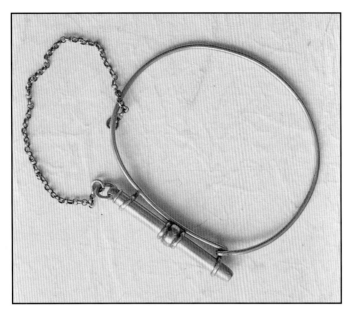

Sterling silver bangle bracelet with a pencil attached, unmarked, circa 1890. $350-$500.

Gun metal and gold retractable pencil with cabochon turquoise stones, on a chain with a gun metal match safe and heart-shaped coin holder. Circa 1880, $650-$725.

Snake pencil.

Gold slide pencil, hand engraved pierced work over sapphire blue enamel, registration mark, with amethyst set in finial. 2 3/4" extended. $625-$750. Hand engraved gold slide pencil with teardrop-shaped cabochon rubies, marked "S. Mordan & Co.," with chalcedony stone set in finial. 2 1/4" closed. $750-$925. On a rolled gold watch chain, 18". $75-$125.

Chains, Lockets, Chatelaines, Belts, Scarf Pins

Book chain and locket.

Book chain and locket.

Detail of locket.

Detail of locket

Silver book chain and locket on a drop.

Long silver chain with heart-shaped slider with knick-set cabochon turquoise.

Long gold chain with hand clasp.

Gold chain.

Gun metal chain. 60" $275-$350. Courtesy of Rachel Marks Antiques.

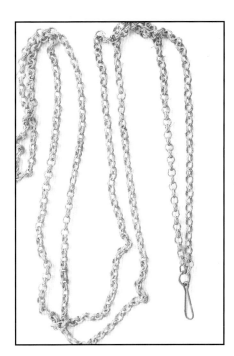

Grass or horse hair chain. $275-$350. *Courtesy of Rachel Marks Antiques.*

Gun metal chain with locket. $275-$350.

Rose gold chain.

Chain with magic pencil. $600+ in mint condition.

Gold and Niello chain. $175-$250.

Gold chain, low karat, tarnishes and may be polished.

Same chain, cleaned.

Brass necklace with gold wash, original ochre patina in recesses. Five daisy with open leaf pendants and drops, die stamped, patterned link chain. Circa 1890. $125-$150.

Brass necklace with twelve double-sided, die stamped pendants dangling from chains of two different lengths. Every other link is patterned. Circa 1890. $125-$150.

Gold plated pendant (die stamped and fabricated) on herringbone chain, with cornucopia spacers. Circa 1880. $125-$150.

Necklace, Russian gold with gold beads and amethyst drops. $1,800-$2,000. *Courtesy of Adele Golden, The Garden Gate Antiques.*

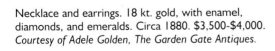

Necklace and earrings. 18 kt. gold, with enamel, diamonds, and emeralds. Circa 1880. $3,500-$4,000. *Courtesy of Adele Golden, The Garden Gate Antiques.*

Gold watch fob in the form of a grotesque, with a diamond in the mouth and original 15 carat chain. *Private collection*. NP (no price).

Locket. Sterling silver. $175-$250. *Courtesy Rachel Marks Antiques.*

Gold drop with three opals, circa 1880. $175-225.

Pansy. Gold with diamond chip locket. *Courtesy of Rachel Marks Antiques.* $150-$175.

Locket with medallion. Marked, sterling. $185-$225. *Courtesy Rachel Marks Antiques.*

All in the shape of fleur-de-lis: two color gold with enamel insets ($65), sterling silver with beaded edges and safety clasp ($45-$65), gold with beaded edges, tiny diamonds ($75), gold filled ($30), jade green enamel ($45), rolled gold with appliquéd snake ($50-$75).

Sterling silver clover chatelaine holder, marked Kerr, 1909. $200-$225. *Courtesy of Rachel Marks Antiques.*

Chatelaine holder, silver, crown shaped with a carnelian in the crest. Approximately 1 1/4" x 1", circa 1880. $50-$75.

Reverse of above, Kerr mark.

Rolled gold Art Nouveau style chatelaine holder, circa 1900. $35-$55.

Art Nouveau sterling silver Unger Bros. chatelaine holder. NP.

"Waitress" pencil and retractable chain in holder, circa 1950. $35-$55.

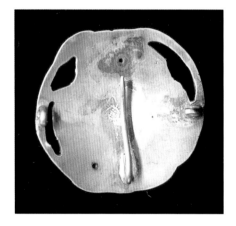

Reverse of above.

Chatelaine with ship. *Courtesy Rachel Marks Antiques.* $300-$400.

Gold chatelaine holder with diamond chips, holding a figural pencil. Circa 1880.

Chatelaine holder in the Japanese style, silver with two color gold appliquéd flowers. $250-$300.

"Unger Bros." belt buckle, sterling silver with Egyptian motif. 2 1/2" x 2 3/4", $400-$500. *Courtesy of Rachel Marks Antiques.*

Sterling silver belt buckle with a cupid, circa 1890, 2 1/2" x 1 1/2". Marked with Simons logo (an "S" in a shield) $225-$275. *Courtesy of Rachel Durland.*

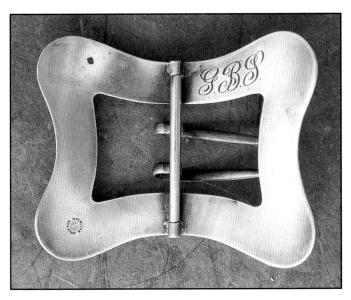

Reverse view of above, showing Unger Brothers logo.

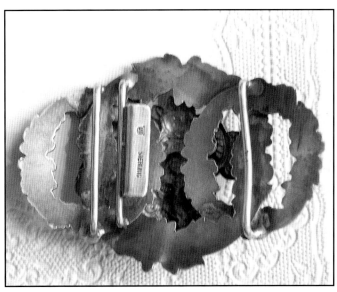

Reverse of belt buckle.

Silver plated belt buckle in the shape of fleur-de-lis, with bezel-set amethysts. Circa 1890, $75-$125.

Sterling silver belt buckle with gold wash, circa 1890, 4" x 2", with faceted green stones in floral bezels and open backs. $175-$225.

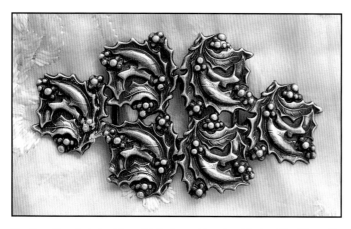

Sterling silver belt buckle, with holly and berries. Marked "La Pierre," 3 1/4" x 1 1/2", $225-$275. *Courtesy of Rachel Marks Antiques.*

Sterling silver belt buckle with grotesques, circa 1890. $75-$125.

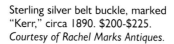

Sterling silver belt buckle, marked "Kerr," circa 1890. $200-$225. *Courtesy of Rachel Marks Antiques.*

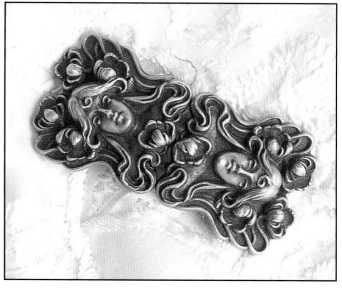

Sterling silver with gold wash, belt buckle with Kerr mark (#579). Two Art Nouveau women, 2 3/4" x 1 1/4", $245-$300. *Courtesy of Rachel Marks Antiques.*

Sterling silver belt buckle with grotesques and putti, with Kerr mark, 3 3/4" x 2 1/4", circa 1890. $300-$350. *Courtesy of Rachel Marks Antiques.*

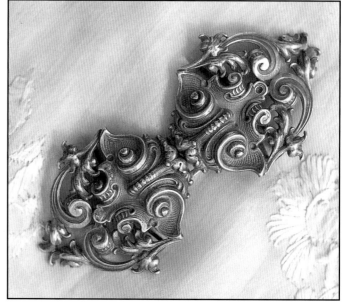

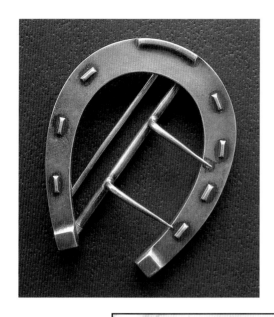

Belt buckle in the shape of a horse shoe. Sterling silver, with Gorham mark. Circa 1870. $225-$275.

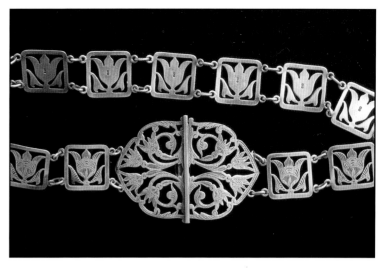

Sterling silver belt, Arts and Crafts (English), 25", $350-$425. *Courtesy of Rachel Marks Antiques.*

Sterling silver belt buckle, 3" x 2", $75-$100. *Courtesy of Rachel Marks Antiques.*

Detail of sterling silver buckle.

Reverse of sterling silver belt buckle.

Art Nouveau belt in sterling silver, 25", marked Kerr, with repoussé irises. $1,250-$1,500. *Courtesy of Rachel Marks Antiques.*

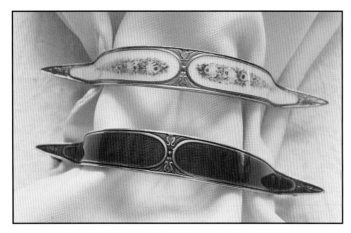

Guilloche enamel, gold washed sterling silver posy holder/scarf pins. Marked with Blackinton logo, 1890-1910, 3" x 1 1/4". $125-$150.

Stick pins (also called scarf pins), circa 1900. Both gold, both with seed pearls in the center. The clover is done in enamel, with considerable detail considering the size (marked "14 K." with a cross). $75-$95.

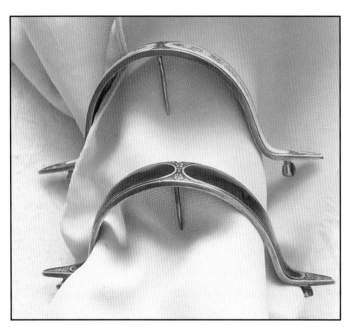

Detail of previous items, showing silver spike.

Stick pin, sterling silver in the Art Nouveau style, circa 1900. $55-$75.

Engraved sterling silver posy holder/scarf pin. 2" x 1". $50-$75.
Sterling silver posy holder/scarf ring, 2" x 3/4". $50-$75.

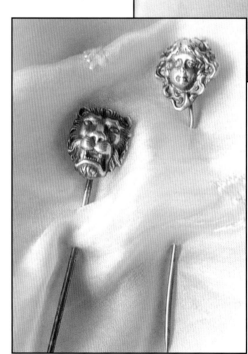

Silver stick pins. $40-$60 each. *Courtesy of Rachel Marks Antiques.*

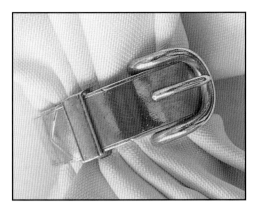

Gold filled scarf ring in the shape of a belt and buckle. Circa 1890, 1" x 1/2". $125-$150.

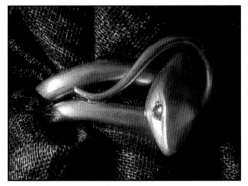

Art Nouveau gold scarf ring in the shape of a serpent with red stone eyes. Hallmarked. $550-$750.

Snake necklace and bracelet. *Courtesy of Rachel Marks Antiques.* $1150-$1250 each.

Detail of above.

Sterling Silver snake pin with green stone eyes and tongue. Four leaf clover mark (Parks). *Private collection.* NP (no price).

Sterling silver vest pocket pencil made by "Edward Todd," circa 1900. $600-$700.

Costume Jewelry

*N*ineteenth century lust for luxury, the quest for affordable beauty, and elegance for the entrepreneurial class, the sense of limitless expansion, and infinitely replenishing natural resources, the almost alchemist-like belief in the ability of man to discover a way to make gold out of a lesser metal, to make something into something else. If not gold, then gold plate! Pearls? Mother-of-pearl. Coral, tortoise-shell or ivory? Celluloid. Horn? Ebonite. Silver? Aluminum. Diamonds?

The explorations and inventions, the quest to invent less expensive substitutes for ivory, coral, horn, etc., for pearls and diamonds and gold and silver — a bit like alchemy but with results that are less magic and more real, less replacement and more re-creation. The search for the novel, the new, the unexpected, and the different was juxtaposed with the perceived need to stay within the boundaries created by social arbiters and their rules of etiquette.

The desire to emulate the acquisitiveness of the wealthy keeps the expanding middle-class on the run. As soon as members of the upper classes were wearing a certain type of jewelry, the middle class set about trying to find similar pieces in a more affordable price-range.

It is perhaps not essential but so much fun to read about the master jewelers of the twentieth century, then to see how their designs have been borrowed, copied, transformed into costume jewelry! The more I learn about jewelry, the more blatantly obvious it becomes that there is an intricate web of connections between art, society, high-end jewelry, and costume jewelry. Although I'd like to proclaim that costume jewelry is a great equalizer, a cogent form of democratization, it is evident that costume jewelry would not be anywhere near as popular as it is without not only the approval but the outright enthusiastic embrace of it by affluent, upper class clientele. The difference is that it is available to more people than precious jewelry traditionally had been, because it is more affordable and that, since the mid-nineteenth century, a rising entrepreneurial class has made it a point to emulate those wealthier than they in every way imaginable.

In the mid-nineteenth century, it became possible for this expanding class to afford luxury items, to have the luxury of time to use them, and to flaunt them. Keeping up with the Joneses, so to speak, became a way of life. As I pointed out in *Silver Novelties of the Gilded Age*, novelty items became increasingly essential, at least from a psychological point of view (as an exhibit at the Newark Museum so aptly phrased it, these items became "Needless Necessities"). In addition to having the economic means necessary to purchase things that in the past would have been deemed frivolous, this entrepreneurial class also sought to emulate the lifestyle of the, well, rich and famous. Conspicuous consumption became de riguer, essentially imbedded in our culture.

Keeping up with the Joneses, though, must have originated with keeping up with the Vanderbilt's, or at least trying to.

Jewelry made of non-precious metals and stones and fine jewelry have many elements in common. Of course, jewelry is worn to adorn, to decorate, to accentuate, to remember, to proclaim, to suggest, to connect, to comfort, to declare, to challenge, and to belong. Jewelry can convey wealth, taste, power, possession, and connection. It can suggest class, it can attract attention, and it can confirm a flagrant lack of refinement. Costume jewelry has roots in many traditions. Spanning from the *bijouterie* that was created in Bohemia from the mid-nineteenth century into the twentieth century to jewelry that was designed by such twentieth century giants as Jean Schlumberger. According to the Brunialtis (2002, p. 17), some costume jewelry was designed by students who attended the Rhode Island School of Design (RISD). However, costume jewelry was also designed by such renowned jewelers as Marcel Boucher (who worked for Cartier, also creating designs for Mazer and for his own euphoniously named firm), Jean Schlumberger (who designed for Schiaparelli long before he became the chief designer for Tiffany), and Alfred Phillipe (who also worked for William Scheer) for Trifari.

It has been said that designing costume jewelry allows for more freedom because the cost of materials isn't as prohibitive as those used in the making of fine jewelry. This may be true, but if one looks at the work of jewelers like Seaman Schepps, it becomes clear that fine jewelers can be playful and inventive, too.

The following list of costume jewelers is not complete by any means, but it gives a sense of the number of companies that made such jewelry in the twentieth century. As noted earlier, the word "signed" refers to a maker's mark. The jewelry in this section, unless otherwise stated, is all signed. Art, Beau, Boucher,

Castlecliff, Capri, Hattie Carnegie, Cellini, Chanel, Ciner, Cini, Coro, Danecraft, Di Mario, DeNicola, Chr. Dior , Eisenberg, Emmons, Eugene, Florenza, Givenchy, Wendy Gell, Hagler, Har, Miriam Haskell, Hobé, Hollycraft, Iskin, Juliana, JJ, Joseff of Hollywood, Kirk's Folly, Kramer, Krementz, Lisner, Matisse, Margot de Taxco, Mazer (Jomaz), Mimi di N., Monet, Morley-Crimi, Napier, Pauline Rader, Rebajes, Renoir, Robért, Nettie Rosenstein, Sarah Coventry, Schiaparelli, Schreiner, Trifari, TruArt, Van del, Vendome, Vogue, Weiner Handwerk, and Weiss. Signed jewelry is easier to research and is generally considered to be more valuable. However, there is unsigned costume jewelry that is better-made than some that is signed and it requires experience and self-confidence to determine what fits best with your own style and taste.

It is advisable that you learn how to examine a piece of jewelry. Take your time. Using a loupe becomes essential (if you don't need one yet, good for you—but you will need one sooner than you think), so that you can scrutinize both the front and back of the piece. When you examine the front you will look to see if all the stones are in place, if there is damage to the plating, if all the prongs are in place, if enamel is chipped, etc. The back should reveal a mark, if there is one. It's also helpful to make sure that the clasp is secure, and you should check to see if there have been any repairs.

If you have been collecting parts, you will know that some stones may be easily replaced but others will be almost impossible to find. If you know a competent jeweler, you may chose to buy a piece that needs some repair. But something that seems like a real bargain because it is broken may end up costing more than it is worth if it requires a lot of repair.

If you are interested in learning more about costume jewelry, start looking through old magazines and catalogs. Trade publications provide another source of information. From the 1929-1930 *Jobbers' Handbook* I learned that R. Blackinton & Co. made silver novelties (p. 152); Adolf Meller Company imported "genuine and imitation stones suitable for costume jewelry" (p. 153); that T. & R. Jewelry Co. was the "fastest growing rhinestone novelty house in America…anything in rhinestones" (p. 155); Dickson Mfg. Co. sold "colored stone and crystal ornaments for every purpose. Always in keeping with latest styles." Napier was located at 389 Fifth Avenue and sold novelties (and had a factory in Meriden, Connecticut) (p. 181); Paispearl Products sold "essence de orient" (p. 182); William Scheer was located at 75 West 45th Street (NYC) and sold "fine jewelry" (p. 186), and Cohn and Rosenberger manufactured novelties and were listed at 167 Point Street, Providence, RI (p.252). William Scheer was mentioned earlier in this book as a jeweler who was affiliated with Cartier and Van Cleef and Arpels. Cohn and Rosenberger became known as "Coro."

A terrific way to learn about costume jewelry is to interview someone who is well known and well regarded in the business.

Recommended Reading

Marcia Brown, *Signed Beauties of Costume Jewelry*.
Carla and Roberto Brunialti, *A Tribute to America, Costume Jewelry 1935-1950*.
Maryanne Dolan, *Collecting Rhinestone & Colored Jewelry*.
Roseann Ettinger, *Forties & Fifties Popular Jewelry*.
Roseann Ettinger, *Popular Jewelry, 1840-1940*.
Deanna Farneti Cera, *Amazing Gems*.
Lyngerda Kelly and Nancy N. Schiffer, *Costume Jewelry, the Great Pretenders*.
Harrice Simons Miller, *Official Price Guide to Costume Jewelry*.
Jane Mulvagh, *Costume Jewelry in Vogue*.
Fred Rezazadeh, *Costume Jewelry*.
Nancy N. Schiffer, *Costume Jewelry: The Fun of Collecting*.
Nancy N. Schiffer, *Fun Jewelry*.
Nancy N. Schiffer, *Rhinestones!*
http://www.austria.org/oldsite/mar96/hattie.htm
http://www.joseffofhollywood.com/

Far left:
Sterling silver and paste bulldog. Could have been made any time between 1890 and 1930. $175-$300.

Left:
Paul Revere on his horse, white metal and rhinestones. Circa 1930. $50-$75.

Flying bird made of white metal, with rhinestones and a small amount of yellow enamel on beak, 2 1/2" x 2", circa 1930. $25-$45.

Venetian gondolier. Sterling silver, clear diamantes and emerald cut glass sapphires. Circa 1940, $75-$125.

Flying bird, marked sterling silver, pavé-set diamantes. Circa 1940, $75-$100.

Smaller flying bird, marked sterling silver, with a gold wash (vermeil). 1 1/2" x 1 1/4", $45-$55.

Tulips, white metal with gold wash, high quality (hand-cut) baguette glass emeralds and amethysts, channel set glass diamantes. 3" x 2 1/4", circa 1930. $125-$150.

Two sterling silver dancers, circa 1940. $75 each.

Rhinestone necklace, circa 1950. Light and dark blue glass stones prong-set. Unmarked, $75-$95.

Marquise clear glass stones set in a white metal brooch, 3 1/2" x 2", circa 1930. $45-$65.

Rhinestone necklace, with iridescent clear stones and black faceted teardrops, prong-set. Unmarked, circa 1950, $75-$95.

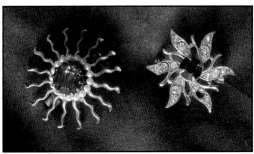

Two rhinestone pins, circa 1940. $25-$45.

Pink rhinestone choker, circa 1950. Unmarked, $65-$75.

Green and clear glass stones set as a bunch of flowers. 3" x 2 1/2", circa 1940. $45-$65.

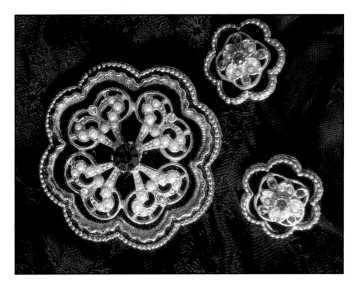

"Art ©" brooch (can be worn as a pendant) and earrings. Gold wash over base metal, with prong-set, faceted citrine stones , faux pearls, diamantes, and turquoise. Circa 1960, brooch approximately 2", $125-$150.

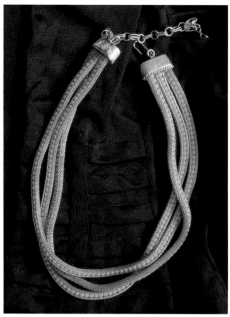

"Capri" artificial turquoise and gold mesh choker, circa 1950. $75-$125.

"© Boucher" mussel shell, gold washed with faux coral cabochons. Circa 1960, 2 1/4" x 1 1/4". $125-$150.

"Alice Caviness" earrings. Circa 1960, $50.

Unmarked brooch and earrings, with gold wash and faux turquoise and pearls. Circa 1960, $75-$95 set.

"Castlecliff" faux pearl (and diamond roundel spacers) necklace. Circa 1950, 14" x 1/4", $50-$75.

Signed "Hattie © Carnegie" brooch, with opaque black (round and faceted) and translucent tortoiseshell glass beads cascading from gold washed leaves. Circa 1955, 2 1/2" x 4". $125-$150.

"Hattie Carnegie" chandelier earrings, 2 1/2". Circa 1950, $45-$65.

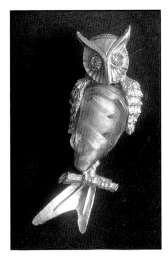

"Hattie Carnegie" fur clip in the shape of an owl. Pink Murano glass body and faceted pink stone eyes, gold wash over white metal. Circa 1950, 2 1/4" x 3/4", $175-$225.

Sterling silver initial rings, marked "Cellini." Circa 1960, $25-$35 each.

"Hattie Carnegie" signed woodpecker trembler. Gold plated tree trunk with a red, white, pink, and light blue enamel woodpecker, with pavé rhinestones. Circa 1950, $150-$225.

"© Chanel®" earrings. The earrings are composed of square, bezel-set mother-of-pearl and two large crystals set in gold colored metal. Circa 1970, $150-$175.

"Hattie Carnegie" trembler earrings. Gold plated clip earrings (2" x 1 1/2") with topaz colored stones. The eight petaled flowers are attached with tiny springs and tremble with any movement. Circa 1940, $150-$175.

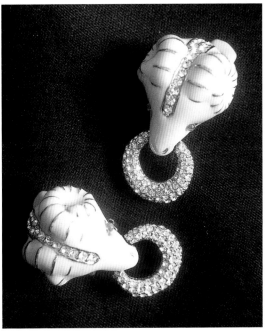

"Ciner" ram's head earrings. White enamel, faceted glass stones. Circa 1960, $45-$55.

Sterling silver pin, made by "Cini" in the 1940s ("Sterling by Cini"). A diminutive frog sits on lily pads, with a pond lily blooming next to him. 2 1/2" x 1 1/2", $250-$325.

"Coro" brooch in the "atomic" style. Black cold enamel on white metal, with amber colored glass prong-set stones, 2 1/4". Circa 1950, $45-$55.

"Coro" Queen holding a flower, wearing a rhinestone crown and a round ruby and square sapphire glass stone necklace. Circa 1950, 1 1/2" x 1 1/4", $75-$95.

"© Corocraft" demi-parure, with yellow and white gold wash, marcasite, and genuine pearls. Brooch: 2", earrings 3/4", circa 1960, $150-$175.

"Coro" charm bracelet, with a heart and key, windmill, wishing well, ballet slippers, and turquoise colored glass beads. Circa 1950, $175-$200.

"© Coro" brooch in the shape of a flower. Gold wash, clear cut-glass stones, 2", circa 1960. $35-$55.

"Corocraft Duette" brooch, $300-$400. *Courtesy of Ruth Taylor.*

"Coro" vermeil earrings and brooch, retro style. Circa 1940, $45-$65.

"Corocraft" cuff bracelet with faux cabochon rubies, emeralds, sapphires, and diamonds, circa 1940. $450-$600. *Courtesy of Ruth Taylor.*

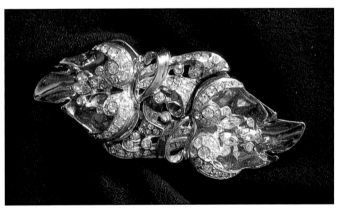

Signed "Corocraft Sterling, patent #1798867" with rose gold wash, duette (brooch convertible into two fur clips). Circa 1940, $175-$225.

"Coro" dress clips, circa 1930. Burnished gold finish, with cabochon ruby red stones in the centers of flowers. Clips 2" long, bracelet 1" wide, $75-$125. Joseff of Hollywood made a similar bracelet.

Two brooches, with flowers that tremble. Marked "Coro" with patent number D117802. Cold enamel, channel set emerald cut green glass stones, and round diamantes. Without Duette brooch, $50-$75.

"CoroDuette" in vermeil, with pavé rhinestones and sapphire blue cabochons, 3" x 1 1/2" as a brooch, 1 1/2" each as a separate dress clip. Circa 1940, $225-$250.

"Cracker Jack charms." $5-$75.

"Di Mario N. Y." brooch, with gilded filigree, faux baroque and seed pearls. 2 1/2" x 1 1/2", circa 1950. Note similarity with Miriam Haskell jewelry. $150-$175.

"Chr. Dior 1965, Germany" flexible gold colored necklace with simulated moonstone, amethyst, and turquoise cabochons, prong-set. $350-$425.

"DeNicola" brooch. A playful version of a kitty cat with an orange face and gold-washed nose, whiskers, eyes (with long lashes), and ears. 1 1/2" x 1 1/2", circa 1960. $65-$75.

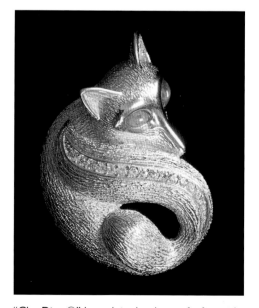

"Chr. Dior ©" brooch in the shape of a fox with his tail curled over his shoulder. Clear cut glass stones inset in tail, green glass stone eyes (with a moonstone effect). 2" x 1 1/2", circa 1970, $75-$150.

"Christian Dior ©" chandelier earrings, circa 1980. Gold plated white metal with clear rhinestones and bezel set red and amber glass emerald-cut stones. 3 1/4" x 1", $125-$150.

Unmarked choker, baroque pearls, cluster with diamantes, faux pearls, roses montees, and the same clover leaves as in the marked "Eugene" earrings. Circa 1940, $175-$225.

"Eisenberg" ring in its original box, circa 1960. $125-$150.

"Florenza ©" brooch, with faux turquoise, pearls, and cameo. 1 1/2" x 1 1/4", circa 1960. $55-$65.

Reverse of brooch/necklace.

"Eugene" earrings. Faux pearls, round and teardrop brilliants, rose gold gilded clover leaf and vine. Circa 1940, $55-$65.

"Florenza" brooch/necklace, circa 1960. N.P. *Courtesy of Kathy Milliken.*

"Florenza ©" bracelet, circa 1960, 7" x 1/2", gold washed, with jade green and iridescent marquise shaped cabochons. $55-$65.

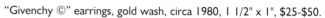

"Givenchy ©" earrings, gold wash, circa 1980, 1 1/2" x 1", $25-$50.

"Florenza ©" mechanical pencil and base. The pencil (4 1/4" x 1/2")is banded with prong-set faux turquoise, rubies, and seed pearls alternating with simulated cording. The terminal is in the form of a crown, topped with red glass stones. The base (1 1/2" x 3/4") is cushion shaped with three tassels as feet. Circa 1955, $150-$175.

Hagler earrings.

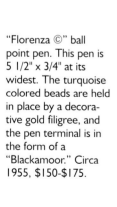

"Florenza ©" ball point pen. This pen is 5 1/2" x 3/4" at its widest. The turquoise colored beads are held in place by a decorative gold filigree, and the pen terminal is in the form of a "Blackamoor." Circa 1955, $150-$175.

"Har ©" brooch in the shape of an insect, gold wash, pavé-set diamantes, red glass stone eyes. 1 1/2" x 2", circa 1960. $45-$65.

Signed "Miriam Haskell," marked on oval tag, string of baroque faux pearls. $125-$150.

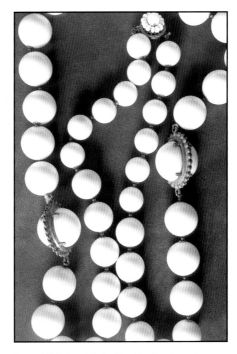

Signed "Miriam Haskell" white beads and gilded brass filigree. With earrings, $125-$150.

Unsigned parure with characteristics that may allow it to be attributed to Miriam Haskel. Circa 1940. $350-$425.

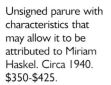

Earrings to match necklace.

Signed "Miriam Haskell" necklace, marked on oval tag, pâte de verre and filigree gold over brass. $125-$150.

Signed "Miriam Haskell" jade colored glass beads with twisted chain. 34", $75-$100.

Signed "Miriam Haskell" rose colored pâte de verre beads in free-form shapes, each hand knotted with faceted silver and rose colored glass bead spacers. 32", $125-$150.

Signed "Miriam Haskell" earrings, blue stones. $55-$75.

Signed "Miriam Haskell" parure: white pâte de verre beads, and flowers painted on larger beads. Necklace: 30", bracelet 7", earrings 1". $250-$325.

Marked "Miriam Haskell" stick pin with baroque faux pearl, rose montees, pansy-shaped clasp. $75-$125.

Signed "Miriam Haskell" stick pin, marked on back. $75-$100.

Signed "Miriam Haskell" demi parure with melon pâte de verre beads, rose montees, silver filigree, and diamante roundels. $350-$425.

Unsigned "Miriam Haskell." See Pamlicov. White pate de verre and green bead lily of the valley brooch. $175-$225.

Signed "Miriam Haskell" coral colored beads with faceted metal spacers, 16", $75-$100.

Earrings. "Miriam Haskell." Turquoise pate de verre. $350-$425.

Signed "Miriam Haskell" necklace (and earrings). Coral colored pâte de verre, gilded filigree pendant with coral colored stones. $750-$825 (with earrings).

Unmarked Haskell brooch, with Roman gold morning glories (as in previous necklace) and dangling brown glass and gilded flowers. $250-$325.

Detail of pendant.

Signed "Miriam Haskell" necklace.

"Miriam Haskell" parure consisting of a necklace, bracelet, earrings, and brooch. Yellow pâte de verre rectangular stones mounted with filigree, and round and faceted beads, which are interspersed with seed beads. Circa 1960, $450-$575.

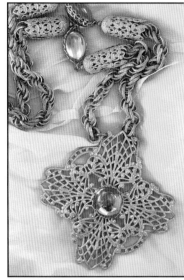

Signed Haskell Maltese cross in Roman gold filigree with amethyst glass stones. Circa 1960, chain 32", cross 3 1/2", $125-$175.

Detail of necklace.

"Miriam Haskell" charm bracelet. Circa 1960, Roman gold finish, with smoky topaz crystals, $175-$225.

Signed "Miriam Haskell" lime green glass beads with filigree and faceted spacers, green cut glass stones on filigree clasp, 16". $125-$175.

Signed "Miriam Haskell" earrings, Roman gold finish on the leaves with diamante, circa 1960. $55-$65.

"Miriam Haskell" brooch in Roman gold with irregularly shaped green pâte de verre stones and beads. Circa 1950, 3 1/2" x 1 1/2", $375-$425.

Signed "Miriam Haskell" brooch. Roman gold finish on the leaves, topaz cut glass stones, circa 1960. $75-$125.

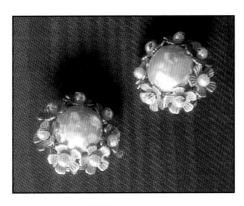

Signed "Haskell" button earrings, circa 1980. Central baroque pearl is surrounded by tiny gold daisies with faux seed pearl centers. 3/4", $65-$75.

"Miriam Haskell" earrings with baroque and seed faux pearls, 2", circa 1940. $125-$150.

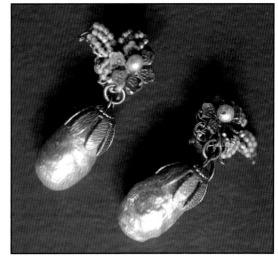

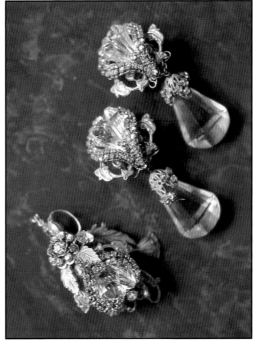

Signed "Miriam Haskell" necklace with gold-capped baroque pearls, and large tooth-shaped essence-of-pearl layered beads. Circa 1940, 16". $250-$300.

"Miriam Haskell' demi-parure in Roman gold, diamantes, crystals. Earrings are 2 3/4" and the brooch is 2 1/2" x 1 1/4". Circa 1950, $375-$425.

243

"Hobé" bracelet, sterling silver and vermeil. Each section is hand-fabricated, and slightly different. Circa 1940, 1 1/4" x 7", $250-$450.

"Hollycraft, Pat. 1958" brooch with iridescent clear cut glass stones. 3" x 1 1/2", $75-$125. Hollycraft dated its jewelry, which is very helpful!

"©J J" brooch. Gold plated white metal of a cat watching goldfish through the fishbowl. Circa 1960, 1 1/2" x 2", $35-$45.

Signed "Joseff" earrings (snakes). Exactly like earrings Elizabeth Taylor wore in the movie *Cleopatra*. $250-$325.

"Juliana" (not signed) style bracelet, 7" x 1 1/2". Opaque white cabochons with colorful (some iridescent) faceted glass stones in fuchsia, green, blue, pink, and orange. Circa 1950. $75-$100.

"Joseff" owl earrings. 2 1/2" x 1 1/2", circa 1940. $250-$275.

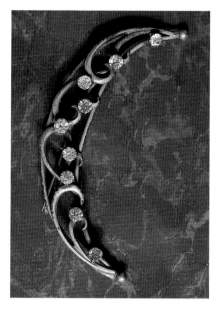

"Joseff" crescent pin, with clear rhinestones. Circa 1940, 3 1/2" x 3/4", $225-$275.

"Kramer of New York" rhinestone choker, circa 1950. $125-$150.

Signed "Joseff" camel brooch. Roman gold finish with both faceted and cabochon stones, circa 1940, 3" x 2 1/2". $375-$450.

Earrings. These "Kramer" earrings were inspired by an original design created by Harry Winston; however, those were diamonds while these are rhinestones. $75-$85.

"Kirk's Folly" brooch, with putti, hearts, moon faces. Circa 1980, 2 1/2" x 1 1/2". $45-$65.

"Kramer©" earrings. White pâte de verre prong set stones, white and gold luster enamel metal leaves. Circa 1950, $25-$35. Kramer is known to have made jewelry for Christian Dior.

"Krementz" genuine opal and rolled-gold brooch in its original box with labels. Circa 1950. $75-$95.

Blue butterfly brooch with opaque blue stones. Kenneth Lane. $175-250.

Gold-washed necklace with Chinese butterfly pendant. Circa 1960, $75-$125.

Signed "©KJL," this 3 3/4" brooch embodies flashy and trashy. With teardrop-shaped faceted fuchsia stones radiating outwards towards marquis-shaped faceted tangerine stones, with translucent pink and coral cabochons and iridescent teardrops, a brooch couldn't be more eye-catching. When I told Mr. Lane the title of this book during our interview, he cheerfully proclaimed "Well, I am trashy!" $75-$150.

Signed "Kenneth Lane ©" cast plastic butterfly (simulated jade) pendant, 3 1/2" x 3", with gold-washed tassel and chain. Circa 1965, $45-$65.

This demi-parure exemplifies the classy in Kenneth Lane's jewelry. Four strands of hand-knotted faux pearls are joined by a 1 1/4" emerald-cut sapphire glass stone surrounded by clear rhinestones. Signed "©KJL," circa 1970, with matching earrings, $250-$325.

Bracelet. Early Kenneth Lane, inspired by medieval jewelry. $450-$550.

Signed "KJL©" pierced earrings, 2 1/4" long with prong-set clear and smoky rhinestones. Circa 1960, $150-$175.

Signed "KJL ©" demi-parure with red, lapis blue, cadmium orange, and turquoise blue beads gathered with gold washed spacers (32"), pendant in the Egyptian style (4"). Earrings with coiled snakes, bead drops. Circa 1960, $325-$425.

Signed "©Kenneth Lane" necklace composed of layers of prong-set, faceted glass stones in a variety of shapes. Rhinestone chain 16", pendant 3 1/2". Circa 1960, $375-$425.

Signed "KJL ©" gold washed bib necklace, 14" x 4". Circa 1970, $250-$375.

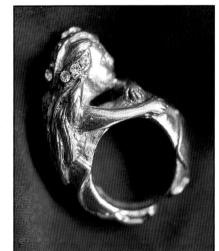

Signed "KJL©" ring, circa 1960. Inspired by Renaissance jewelry. $55-$75.

Signed "KJL©" bracelet, shaped like shells. Circa 1970, $125-$150.

"Margot de Taxco" #5385 (or 0), handcrafted demi-parure consisting of a brooch and earrings. Pale blue enamel over stippled pattern, brooch is 2 1/2" x 1 1/2". Circa 1940, $375-$450.

Signed "Matisse" earrings and brooch, made of copper with green mottled enamel in the shape of leaves and tendrils. Large "Renoir" copper brooch with turquoise, black, and gold enamel. Circa 1950, $45-$75.

"© Lisner" brooch, with textured metal, gold wash, and six cultured pearls. 2", circa 1960. $75-$100.

"Mazer" brooch. White metal, with carved blue stones and brilliants, in the giardinari style. Circa 1930, $325-$425.

"Jomaz©" cocktail ring, with turquoise colored cabochon, pavé pastes and gold accents. With a dome over 1/2" high, this ring makes a statement. Circa 1960,

"Jomaz©" Demi-parure with brushed yellow gold-plated metal, white gold settings for the pavé set pastes. The bracelet is 1 1/2" wide, the earrings are 2" long. Circa 1960, $175-$225.

"Napier Sterling" brooch in the shape of a highly articulated leaf. Matte and shiny gold finish, cultured pearl. 2" x 1 1/2", circa 1945, $75-$95.

Attributed to Pauline Rader, Chinese dragon brooch. 3" x 2", gold-plated, with enamel, pavé set rhinestones, black cabochon stones along the spine and red cabochon eyes. Circa 1950, $75-$95.

"Morley-Crimi Hand-wrought" copper necklace, stylized calla lilies in a repeat pattern. Circa 1950, 16", $75-$95.

Signed "Pauline Rader" moth, tremblant. Gilded metal with faux baroque pearl body, green stone eyes, and pavé rhinestones. Circa 1960, $175-$250.

Signed "Rebajes" copper pendant, with stylized leaves. Circa 1950, $75-$95. *Courtesy Maris Durland.*

Sterling silver "Rebajes" brooch with flowers, 2 1/4" x 2 1/2". Circa 1950, $75-$125. *Courtesy Maris Durland.*

Signed "Rebajes" copper brooch in the shape of a flying bird, flat and textures, hammer marks evident on wings. 2 1/4" x 2 1/2", circa 1950. $75-$95. Both of these designs were also made by Rebajes in silver. *Courtesy Maris Durland.*

Signed "Rebajes" copper brooch with masks of tragedy and comedy, 2 1/2" x 2". Circa 1950, $150-$175. *Courtesy Maris Durland.*

"Rebajes" Chihuahua, hand-fabricated, 2" x 2", circa 1950, $75-$125. Anonymous poodle, machine stamped, $15-$25. *Courtesy Maris Durland.*

Signed "Rebajes" copper brooch, in the modern style. Circa 1950, $150-$175. *Courtesy Maris Durland.*

Signed "Rebajes" sterling silver earrings, stylized faces with a wave and a curl for hair. Circa 1950, 1 1/4" x 3/4". $55-$75. *Courtesy Maris Durland.*

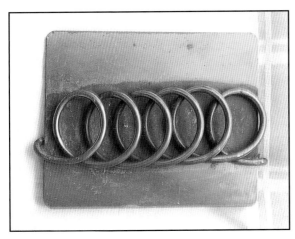

"Rebajes" brooch with appliquéd wire loops. Circa 1950, $55-$75. *Courtesy Maris Durland.*

"Rebajes" necklace, overlapping copper segments shaped like leaves, 16" x 3/4". $75-$125. *Courtesy Maris Durland.*

"Rebajes" copper cuff bracelet. Circa 1950, $125-$150. *Courtesy Maris Durland.*

"Rebajes" copper and red enamel necklace. Unusual. $175-$225. *Courtesy Maris Durland.*

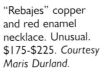

Detail of copper cuff bracelet, Rebajes signature.

Signed "Original by Robért." Demi-parure of brooch/pendant and ear clips, with simulated pearls and seed pearls, prong set diamantes, and opalescent pâte de verre stones in teardrop shapes, with gilded flowers, all hand-set into filigree base. Set, $175-$225.

"Nettie Rosenstein" butterfly, tremblant. Gold wash with pavé-set diamantes. 2 1/2" x 1 1/2", circa 1950. $225-$275.

"Nettie Rosenstein" many shades of blue, clear glass, and pâte de verre, double strand. Circa 1950, $125-$175.

"Schiaparelli" necklace, circa 1950. Not a very dramatic piece, however, it does have the original label. The pink label, in the shape of a manne-quin, says "Schiaparelli Jewels" on one side, and "Designed in Paris, created in America" on the other. This tag indicates that the piece was made after 1949, when the Schiaparelli name was licensed in the United States. Three strands of matte white plastic beads, approximately 21". $45-$65.

"Schiaparelli" demi-parure. Necklace and earrings with opaque white pâte de verre stones, irides-cent molded leaves and faceted stones. Circa 1945, $325-$400.

"Schiaparelli" bracelet, with a gold wash and channel-set calibre cut glass stones. Circa 1950, $150-$175.

"Schiaparelli" shocking pink, from a box of stationary, circa 1940.

"Schiaparelli" watch and large link chain. N.P.

252

"Schiaparelli" earrings. N.P.

Watermelon earrings, signed "Schiaparelli." 1 1/4", circa 1950, $50-$75.

Women on a swing. Jean Schlumberger designed a necklace with these die stamped images. $75-$125.

"Schreiner" brooch, with emerald, marquise, round, and square clear cut glass stones on a raised setting (2" square, 1" deep.). The stones are very well cut and highly reflective. Circa 1955, $250-$325.

"Shreiner" brooch. $275-$375.

Orchid. "Trifari". Marked "TF". Trembler. $650-$750.

"Trifari Design Patent No. 155187" key brooch, circa 1955. 2 3/4" x 1", gold wash, faux rubies, diamantes, enamel. $175-$225.

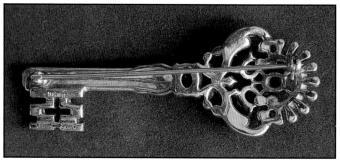

"Trifari" (with a crown over the T), two dragons. Fur clip, 2" x 1 1/2", circa 1940, $65-$75.

Reverse of preceding photograph.

"Trifari" blue bird, with cold enamel and simulated cabochon ruby eye. Circa 1960, 1 1/2" x 1", $65-$75.

Reverse of blue bird.

"Trifari" beaded necklace, with fringe. Opaque black glass beads, faceted, with gilded metal melon spacers and bronze colored filigree and beaten beads. 26" with 3" fringe. Circa 1940, $75-$125.

"Necklace and earrings, signed "Trifari." Gold plated chains with tassel, vibrant blue and pink faceted glass stones prong-set on hollow round forms. Necklace 26" with 2 1/2" tassel. Circa 1960, $125-$175.

"Vendôme" earrings. Enamel bananas and leaves, with cut glass citrines, prong-set. 1 1/4" x 1/2", circa 1950. $25-$35.

"Vogue" earrings. Black faceted aurora borealis beads on chains that move. Circa 1950, $75-$95.

"TruArt" vermeil brooch in the form of a bunch of flowers with marquise cut and round cut glass citrines. 2" x 2", circa 1940. $65-$95.

"Vendome" brooch with white and green paté de verre disks, black beads, turquoise colored pâte de verre flowers, and iridescent faceted cut glass beads wired on filigree metal back. Circa 1940, 2", $75-$95.

"Weiner Handwerk" necklace, with original label. Sterling silver and enamel in violet and pink, with cloisonné. Pendant measures 1 5/8" x 1 1/8", 18" chain with fine, rectangular links. $75-$125.

"Weiss" bug in aurora borealis and black enamel. Circa 1950, $55-$75.

Brooch in the shape of horse chestnuts. Gold plated metal and brown glass beads. Circa 1940, 2" x 1 1/2". $25-$40.

Dress clip, gold plated with overlapping leaf pattern. Circa 1940, $45-$55.

"Weiss" bracelet with original tag, pansy brooch, and earrings. Circa 1950. Bracelet, $65-$75. Earrings and brooch, $75-$125.

Archeological revival belt buckle. Dolphins frolic around the Greek youth (with a classic profile) and inspire a stylized design on each side of the imitation coin. Gold plated, with glass am-ethysts, circa 1890. 4 1/2" x 2". $75-$95.

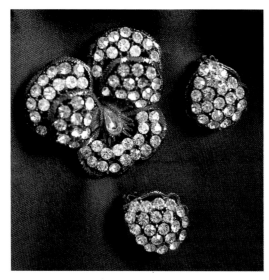

"Weiss" pansy brooch and earrings, with blackened metal and two shades of pink cut glass stones. $75-$125.

Art Deco necklace in orange and black.

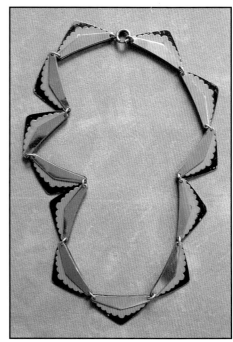

Necklace with turquoise glass cabochons, lapis lazuli, cobalt blue enamel, and pearls
Set in flat and domed gold filigree, the stones and enamel create a stunning effect. 14" x 1 1/2".
Circa 1950, $350-$425.

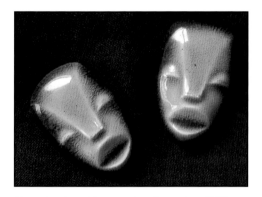

Ceramic pins with turquoise glaze, circa 1950. $25-$40 pair.

Beaded necklace and earrings.

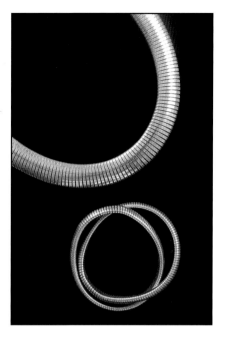

Silver necklace and double bracelet.

Unmarked brooch (converts to a pendant) in the shape of a shaggy dog's head, with movable gold-tone chains fur, and prong-set faceted stones features. Circa 1960, 2 1/2" x 3 1/2", $75-$95.

Turquoise glass beads with granulated gold beads, beautifully made but unmarked. 28", circa 1950, $45-$55.

Unsigned brooch, Victorian stick-pin revival, circa 1970. $35-$65.

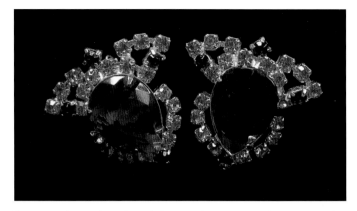

Earrings with tear-drop shaped glass amethyst stones and prong-set pink and purple faceted glass stones. 1 1/2" x 1 1/2". Circa 1950, $15-$20.

White metal brooch with white and lavender cold enamel and rhinestones. Unmarked, circa 1930. $75-$125.

Bug pin and earrings.

Unsigned brooch in the shape of a starfish with various sea-life dangles. Gold finish, faux coral and pearls. 3" circumference. Circa 1960, $35-$55.

Asian inspired demi-parure with necklace and earrings. Unmarked, circa 1940, faux pearls and jade cabochons, with movable hoop earrings on all three people. $175-$225.

Unsigned brooch in the shape of a branch with leaves and purple glass dangles. $25-$35.

Summer white brooch. Unsigned. $25-$45.

White Pate de verre with glass leaves, French. $275-$350.

Summer white brooch. Unsigned. $25-$45.

Clip earrings. A part shows in front of the ear with the marquis shaped stones and the rest shows on the back. Unsigned. Goes with necklace. $5-$10.

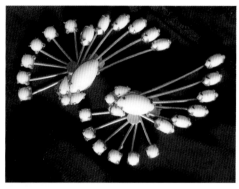

Necklace with ivory colored glass and vermeil beads (marked "Hecho Mexico"). Circa 1960, 32" with a 4" pendent, $75-$125.

Summery white necklace with poured white glass marquis shaped bead prong set. $25-$35.

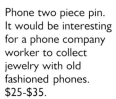

Phone two piece pin. It would be interesting for a phone company worker to collect jewelry with old fashioned phones. $25-$35.

Unsigned demi-perure gold plated metal with pearls. $25-$45.

Grape cluster faux pearl. N.P.

Unmarked White metal brooch, with cold enamel stem and pink and white rhinestones, en tremblant. Circa 1930.Replaced pin. $55-$75.

Large 3 1/2" circumference plastic Made in Japan brooch with light and dark blues. $15-$25.

Butterfly earrings. A spectacular 5 inches long, each earring is set with more than 215 clear rhinestones. White metal, clips, circa 1950. $350-$425. Unsigned.

Unsigned choker with light blue flowers, plastic with gilded chain, circa 1940. $45-$65.

Sterling silver crown brooch, circa 1940. Prong-set faceted glass sapphire, aquamarine, ruby stones, with green, amber, pink, red cabochons and rhinestones. 2" x 2". $75-$125.

Brilliant blue stones with unusual prongs make this unmarked demi-parure an eye-catcher. $75-$100.

Brooch, contemporary (from vintage parts).

Brooch in the shape of a dragon. Similar to dragon jewelry made by Har, this 3" x 2" piece is not signed (but is perhaps made by Art). $175-$225.

White metal trembler (notice tiny spring), orchid shape with clear and green glass stones, 2" x 1 3/4". Circa 1940, $55-$75.

Silver pin with red enamel, hand made Scottie dog, circa 1950. $35-$45.

About Kenneth Jay Lane

Meeting Kenneth Jay Lane was an exciting experience! Here are excerpts from our discussion about jewelry:

Q.: You are able to maintain a balance between playfulness and classicism. What elements of traditional art, sculpture, jewelry, etc., inspire your designs?

A.: All! I just got back from Russia ... ahh, the Hermitage ... [an idea is formed] in the mind and stays there until it somehow oozes out.

Q.: You seem to be able to make what's old new, and what's new immediately classic. There is a continuum in your work, but it is never boring. I'm sure this is an innate talent, but do you have any thoughts on how this happens?

A.: None what-so-ever. It is a part of who I am.

Q.: Do you collect anything?

A.: Nineteenth century Orientalist paintings. I wear a minimum of jewelry. The watch I am wearing was given to me by Micky Mouse (laugh).

Q.: Any recommendations for young art students?

A.: Pay attention to advertising design. Get out of Michigan.

Impressions of the Showroom

It is as if I'm in heaven, a heaven designed and created by a god who is ever-so delighted by the burnished gold, iridescent pearls, corals, turquoises, a god who understands the lust for beauty, a connection with nature embellished with the human touch ... floor to ceiling drawers filled with jewelry, displays showcasing new designs ...

Famous People and Jewelry

It seems that many books about jewelry pay tribute to famous people and their jewelry. Liz Taylor wrote *My Love Affair with Jewelry*. Actresses wear Henry Winston jewelry to the Academy Awards. Bing Crosby and Elvis Presley owned companies that, among other things, produced costume jewelry. Artists Frida Kahlo and Louise Nevelson loved to wear jewelry as a dramatic statement.

Think about Audrey Hepburn's wonderful jewelry in *Breakfast at Tiffany's*. Fulco Verdura designed the jewelry Katherine Hepburn wore in *Philadelphia Story*. The Chanel exhibit at the Metropolitan Museum of Art (Spring 2005) allowed us to ooh and ahh over some stunning bracelets, brooches, and necklaces, and to enjoy the over-the-top Lagerfeld pearls the size of ping-pong balls.

Recommended Reading
Laurie Lisle, *Louise Nevelson, a Passionate Life*.
Axel Madsen, *Chanel, a Woman of Her Own*.
Stefano Papi and Alexandra Rhodes, *Famous Jewelry Collectors*.
Kenneth J. Lane and Harrice Simons Miller, *Faking It*.

Cautions

*I*ronically, when I was about half finished with this book, I became very ill due to the cumulative effects of many, many years of exposure to various chemicals used in art. As an artist, I've been exposed to more chemicals than one might think. The substances that are, to me, the most toxic, are solvents, particularly those used in the process of etching metals. Turpentine, asphaltum, acids, rubber cement, thinners, fumes from kilns and soldering, etc., have taken their toll and I certainly suffered as a result. In addition to severe upper-respiratory illness, I also suffered from something called "chemical intoxication." Don't be mislead by the word "intoxication." This was a most unpleasant experience which included headaches that lasted for months at a time and a peculiar sense of disconnect. It included a variety of side effects that were disorienting and very difficult to deal with. I am lucky to have found several excellent doctors, who were able to diagnose and treat me in such a way that I am now healthy again. It was a long, hard road, though.

My workplace is much safer now, thankfully, and I am much more aware of fumes, etc, and have learned to respond immediately if there are any strong chemical odors. I will always have to be careful around chemicals (and things I used to take for granted, like using certain materials in art, or even having my nails done or wearing perfume, are no longer a part of my life). I am discussing these health and safety issues for two reasons: firstly, to warn others; secondly, to emphasize the warning by drawing attention to direct connections between what happened to me and what happened to jewelers in the past.

There were workers who assembled watches in Waltham, Massachusetts, who were exposed to radiation from the glow-in-the-dark watch faces and who died of cancer as a result. There are jewelers who, because of chemical exposures, find themselves with bladder cancer. Jewelers have long been affected by the materials they work with. It is documented that the leading cause of death for jewelers in Newark, New Jersey (a major center for the production of fine jewelry in the nineteenth century), was upper-respiratory illness (Dietz, p. 143, 1997). Then, as is still often the case, the illness was blamed on the worker rather than the employer. If we are aware, employee and employer together, we can create safe environments that will ultimately increase productivity and we will all be better off as a result.

Jewelers from Newark participated in the very first Labor Day parade, in New York City on September 5, 1882. They joined others who carried signs with such slogans as "All Men Born Equal," "Agitate, Educate, Organize," and "Labor Creates all Wealth" (Dietz, pp. 132-133, 1997). The jewelers of Newark were highly skilled craftsmen who produced fine jewelry, and were recognized with respect. The workforce in New England (particularly in Providence, Rhode Island, and Attleboro, Massachusetts), which produced primarily costume jewelry, consisted largely of unskilled, untrained workers, many of whom were women and children. These workers often suffered long hours and poor working conditions and were also inadequately paid. It seems almost perverse that the production of jewelry that was meant to be appealing, accessible, and affordable to the working classes supported a system in which the workers who made the jewelry were overworked and poorly paid.

Recommended Reading
Michael McCann. *Artist Beware: The Hazards of Working with all Art and Craft Materials and the Precautions Every Artist and Photographer Should Take.*
Charles Lewton-Brain. *The Jewelry Workshop Safety Report.*

Jewelry attracts most of us in the ways it's supposed to. We see what we want and we buy it, either for ourselves or for someone we care about. Dealers know what their customers want and what they can sell, and buy accordingly. Some people, however (and most unfortunately), are attracted to jewelry in a very different way. They don't want to wear it or give it to friends, and they don't want to pay for it. One of the hazards of being a jewelry dealer is being robbed.

I interviewed a couple who have owned an antiques shop in a quaint town along the Hudson River for close to thirty years. Both the husband and the wife are well-regarded, friendly people who seem always ready with a smile. The wife is diminutive, barely five feet tall. One would never imagine that anyone would ever try to hurt her. Yet, she survived a horrendous beating that nearly killed her. Apparently thieves had been watching the store, because they knew exactly what time the husband went out to get lunch, and they knew just when the policeman made his rounds.

They knew that the woman would be alone for fifteen minutes, and that's when they struck.

One man, who appeared to be alone, rang the bell and was admitted. An accomplice immediately followed him in, locked the door, and pulled the shade. The two men pointed a gun at the woman and told her to unlock the cases. Perhaps she was too slow, perhaps she was too resistant, because the thieves began smashing the glass cases. While one robber filled bags with diamond and other expensive jewelry, the other pushed our heroine into a back room and tied her with wire. After she was tied, he pushed her down and started bashing her head on the cement floor. Unsatisfied with that brutality, he tried to garrote her. She was determined to survive and fought back, wiggling and squirming and refusing to give up—a tiny woman against a crazed criminal … her courage served her well, because the man was unable to keep the wire round her neck. The robbers fled after trying to lock her in the back room.

As soon as she heard them leave, she managed to get the door open and crawled across the floor, which was littered with broken glass. She reached the front door just as her husband was returning. Needless to say, he rushed her to the hospital where she was treated for a concussion. The doctors stitched the deep cut in her head and took care of her other wounds. The police responded immediately and were able to track the thieves for a while. The trail ended when the police found the jewelry thieves' abandoned van. In it was a bag filled with over $70,000 worth of diamonds, as well as some loose jewelry. The remainder of the jewelry has not been found, and the robbers have not be caught.

Our brave friend is doing well. Her bangs cover the scar on her forehead, and her husband never leaves her alone in the store. You can bet that security has been tightened. Yet both the wife and husband are still the same kind of people they always have been. The thieves stole jewelry, but they were unable to steal something far more valuable.

Jewelry theft is, of course, not new. We know that thieves entered the pyramids not long after the pharaohs were interred, targeting the gold jewelry that adorned the deceased rulers. European nobility took to wearing paste rather than diamonds when traveling, in an effort to prevent robberies. In America, the Jeweler's Security Alliance was formed as early as 1883 to protect its members from thieves.

In Conclusion, but Not the End

*W*hile I thought I was limiting the topic by focusing primarily on jewelry that was available to the rising middle class in America during a finite time period, I have still found myself in a situation where I will never learn enough about, never photograph enough examples of, and never talk to enough people about this endlessly engaging topic. So, with my publisher's gentle persuasion ("Deb, put what you have in a box and send it to us!"), my editor's kind faith ("Peter, don't give up on her yet."), my friends' and family's persistent inquiries ("Deb, your publisher hasn't given up on you yet?") … I am pulling this together and sending what I have so far. In other words, I will never finish, so I am done for now. On to book number four!

Glossary

Agraffe: hook and eye fastener for a cloak. Often decorative in the nineteenth century.

Aigrette: an ornament worn on the head (in the hair or on a hat), originally imitating a feather.

Ambrotype: photograph on glass, invented in about 1850. The glass plate could act as a positive (rather than negative) image by placing black paper behind it.

Appliqué: applied work.

Archeological style: period between 1850-1890, when there were many archeological discoveries that influenced jewelry design.

Art Deco: started in France during the 1920s and 1930s in reaction to the flowing lines and femininity of Art Nouveau. Name abbreviated from L' Exposition Internationale des Arts Décoratifs, Paris, 1925. Jewelry made in this style may employ an Egyptian, Indian, African, or Chinese influence, hard-edges, and abstract forms.

Art Nouveau: 1890s-1900s. Immediately identifiable as jewelry which incorporates themes from nature (flowers, insects, young women, etc.); stylized, sinuous lines; rounded, asymmetrical forms; and the use of cabochon, often non-precious, stones.

Articulated: in jewelry, this could mean very detailed. Or, it could mean that the jewelry has characteristics that enable it to move, for example the components may be attached with jump rings that allow the torso of an animal to move separately from the head.

Arts and Crafts Movement: Inspired by William Morris, in reaction to machine made, mass-produced ware. Decorative arts were made by hand, inspired by Pre-Raphaelites.

Baroque Pearl: pearl that is not round but rather shaped in an asymmetrical form.

Baguette: rectangular, faceted stone, often a diamond (or rhinestone).

Bail: loop that connects a pendant, charm, etc., to a chain.

Baroque pearl: pearl (real or simulated) that is formed in an unusual, not round, shape.

Basse taille: often referred to as guilloché. Metal is engraved and a transparent enamel overlay allows the design to show through, enamel appears darker where lines are deeper.

Belle Époque: period between 1890-1910.

Bezel: rim of metal that holds a stone in place.

Bijou de couture: jewelry specifically made for a designer, haute couture jewelry.

Bijouterie: jewelry.

Blackamoor: youthful African depicted in jewelry.

Bookchain: term originally described a wide, flat chain with rectangular elements, but the term is now used to describe Victorian chains with elaborate, wide (generally about 1/2") components. While it is essentially comprised of links, the links are not open and as visible as in a typical chain, and the chain is as clearly decorative as is the pendant.

Brevet: French equivalent for "patent."

Brilliant cut: stone cut with many facets.

Cabinet card: larger version of the carte de visite (6 3/4" x 4 1/2"), in use by 1862.

Cabochon: stone cut with a flat bottom and a smooth, domed top.

Calibre: stones cut to fit into specific parts of a piece of jewelry.

Carte de visite: visiting card (2 1/2" x 4 1/2") with a photograph. Became popular in the mid-1850s.

Champlevé: enamel that is set into recesses in metal.

Chasing: metal is moved and repositioned by chiseling with a chasing tool and a mallet.

Chatelaine: holder for many items, which are hung from it by chains. May be hooked onto a belt or worn as a brooch.

Cold enamel: painted enamel (as opposed to glass enamel, which is fired).

Crystal: may mean natural stone, cut glass or the clear glass over a watch-face, depending on context.

Cloisonné: enamel is held in cells or compartments made of wire on top of a metal (silver, gold, etc.) base.

Cultured pearls: pearls are cultivated by introducing a foreign substance (or "seed") into a living oyster.

Daguerreotype: "mirror with a memory." Earliest photographs on silver-plated copper. First images were captured circa 1830.

Deposé: registered mark on pieces exported from or imported into France.

Die-stamping: metal is formed by striking it between two dies. Process of mechanization that allowed mass-production of jewelry.

Diamanté: small cut glass stone that resembles a diamond.

Duette: generally a brooch that can be disassembled to form two other pieces of jewelry.

Ebonite: black hard rubber (see vulcanite).

Engine-turning: Design is created (engraved) on the surface of the metal with a machine, often guided by hand (especially in the nineteenth century).

Engraving: Design is created on the surface of metal by hand, using a sharp tool called a burin.

Essence d'orient: pearl essence. Used to make faux pearls, originally made of fish scales.

Faience: glazed composition (Egyptian paste).

Festoon necklace: Necklace that has a series of pendants or drops hanging from it.

Figural: jewelry made in the shape of a recognizable object. For example, a brooch in the form of a dog.

Filigree: design made out of wire, or stamp-cut to appear to have been made of wire.

Fob: ornamental (sometimes also functional) object attached to a watch chain.

Gilding: thin layer of gold over metal base.

Girandole: earring with pendant shapes (usually three) suspended from the part that adorns the earlobe.

Gorget: flat necklace that rests against breastbone.

Guilloché: enamel over engine-turned metal.

Gutta-percha: similar to black hard rubber or vulcanite, but does not release sulphur odor when rubbed.

Hallmark: mark that verifies quality of metal.

Haute couture: high fashion.

Heracles knot: also called "lover's knot." Interlocking rope form, symmetrical knot with loops in center and the two open ends of either knot facing outwards.

Inclusion: natural flaw in a real stone.

Jabot pin: stick pin.

Jet: dense, coal-like natural substance used for jewelry.

Lava: jewelry made of hardened lava from Mt. Vesuvius, Italian, nineteenth century.

Magic pencil: the mechanism of a magic pencil disappears within the barrel, which is often figural. When one end is pulled, the pencil emerges and is usable, albeit usually for very short notes (the pencil is generally under two inches in length). Invented in the mid nineteenth century and used until about 1930.

Marcasite: iron pyrite, sometimes imitated with cut steel, glass, or plastic.

Marquise: stone is faceted and cut as an ellipse but rather than being rounded, both ends are pointed.

Masonic jewelry: emblems of Freemasons.

Medallion: flat metal shape with embossed face, usually a portrait of a Classical figure.

Mourning jewelry: often black, but sometimes made of hair, worn in memory of a loved one.

Netsuke: ornamental carving attached to inro (small container) worn by Japanese, hung from obi (sash).

Niello: silver is mixed with materials that cause it to permanently oxidize (becoming and remaining black), and is then inset into silver.

Parure: suite of jewelry (brooch, bracelet, necklace, earrings).

Paste: cut lead glass (simulating diamonds). Invented by Ravenscroft (Eng.) and Strass (Fr.).

Pâte de verre: ground glass is made into a paste with a flux and melted again into a mold. Pâte de verre is generally opaque, in any color.

Pavé: stones set so close together as to appear that the metal is "paved" with stones, generally diamonds or simulated diamonds.

Pinchbeck: alloy that simulated gold, invented in the eighteenth century.

Piqué: inlay of mother-of-pearl, silver, or gold into tortoiseshell.

Plique à jour: enamel without a metal support behind it, and is translucent as a result. Held in place by the metal forms around it.

Repoussè: metal is formed by pounding it from the back, creating a raised design.

Retro: style popular in the 1940s and 50s. Modernistic, stylized ribbons, flowers, large stones, often sterling or vermeil.

Rhinestone: originally a natural stone (rock crystal) from Germany. Term now used for any clear stone, white or colored.

Roman finish: matt surface on gold, usually attained by placing the jewelry in acid briefly to remove any alloys in the surface layer.

Rondelle: thin disk or small flat bead that is strung between larger beads.

Roses montées: small clear cut glass stone set into a flower-like metal finding.

Sautior: long necklace or chain.

Sprue: when a piece of jewelry is cast, there has to be a channel for the molted metal to flow into the mold. The sprue is the piece added onto the original (usually made of wax) in order to provide this entry way for the casting material. The sprue is therefore also cast in the process, and it is removed from the piece during the finishing process.

Stanhope: a microphotograph or drawing is attached to a crystal inset in a piece of jewelry (or novelty), and is viewed by holding the image up to a light.

Strass: invented in the early eighteenth century by Georges-Frédéric Strass as an imitation of brilliant, clear precious stones.

Stereoview: From the 1870s up until about 1910, people viewed two, slightly different photographs of the same scene through a stereo viewer, which made the image appear to be three dimensional. Stereoviews are the cards that hold the two photographs.

Suffragette jewelry: at the turn of the twentieth century, jewelry was made using green, violet and white stones, symbolizing the phrase "Give the vote to women."

Tubogas: (gas tube) flexible chain that has an appearance reminiscent of a gas hose. Popularized during the Art Deco era.

Trembler: (also, en tremblant) jewelry that trembles when it moves. Parts are attached with fine springs that allow insect's wings, for example, to move.

Tutti-Frutti: Carved, colorful stones used in Art Deco fine as well as costume jewelry.

Vermeil: gold plated sterling silver.

Vinaigrette: small container used to hold fragrant "vinegar," held to nose to mask unpleasant smells.

Vulcanite: black hard rubber, invented by Charles Goodyear and used in jewelry from 1860-1890. Also called ebonite.

Bibliography

Ackerman, Diane. *A Natural History of Love*. New York: Random House, 1994.

A Short Story of Aluminum from Clay to Cooking Utensil. Manitowoc, Wisconsin: The Aluminum Goods Manufacturing Co., n.d.

Aikins, Ronna Lee. *Brilliant Rhinestones*. Paducah, Kentucky: Collector Books, 2003.

Andrews, Carol. *Amulets of Ancient Egypt*. London: British Museum Press, 1994.

Arnold, Sir Edwin. *Japonica*. New York: Charles Scribner's Sons, 1891.

Art Deco Jewelry Designs. New York: Dover Publications, Inc., 1993.

Baird, Merrily. *Symbols of Japan*. New York: Rizzoli International Publication, Inc., 2001.

Baker, Lillian. *100 Years of Collectible Jewelry*. Paducah, Kentucky: Collector Books, 1978, with 1999 value update.

Baker, Lillian. *Art Nouveau & Art Deco Jewelry, an Identification and Value Guide*. Paducah, Kentucky: Collector Books, 1981, with 1997 value update.

Ball, Joanne Dubbs and Dorothy Hehl Torem. *Masterpieces of Costume Jewelry*. Atglen, Pennsylvania: Schiffer Publishing Ltd., 1996.

Baren, Maurice. *Victorian Shopping*. London: Michael O'Mara Books Limited, 1998.

Bari, Hubert and Violaine Sautter. Translated by Michael Hing. *Diamonds: In the Heart of the Earth, in the Heart of the Stars, in the Heart of Power*. Paris: Vilo International, 2001.

Barry, Kit. *The Advertising Trade Card*. n.p., 1981.

Becker, Ingeborg, and Ulrike von Hase-Schmundt, Christianne Weber. *Theodore Fahrner Jewelry...Between Avant-Gard and Tradition*. West Chester, Pennsylvania: Schiffer Publishing Ltd., 1991.

Becker, Vivienne. *Antique and Twentieth Century Jewelry*. 2nd ed. London: N. A. G. Press, 1997.

Bell, C. Jeanenne. *Collector's Encyclopedia of Hairwork Jewelry*. Paducah, Kentucky: Collector Books, 1998.

Bell, C. Jeanenne. *Answers to Questions About Old Jewelry, 1840-1950*. 5th ed. Iola, Wisconsin: Krause Publications, 1999.

Bell, C. Jeanenne. *How to Be a Jewelry Detective*. Shawnee, Kentucky: A. D. Publishing, 2000.

Bell, C. Jeanenne. *Warman's Antique Jewelry Field Guide*. Iola, Wisconsin: Krause Publications, 2003.

Benjamin, John. *Starting to Collect Antique Jewelry*. Woodbridge, Suffolk, England: Antique Collectors' Club, 2003.

Bird, Isabella. *Unbeaten Tracks in Japan: An Account of Travels on Horseback in the Interior*. New York: G. P. Putnam's Sons, 1880.

Bizot, Chantal, Marie-Noël de Gary, and Évelyne Possémé. *English translation by Alexandra Bonfante-Warren. The Jewels of Jean Schlumberger*. New York: Harry N. Abrams, Inc., 2001.

Bowman, John J. *The Jewelry Engraver's Manual*. New York: D. Van Nostrand Company, Inc., 1954.

Boyd, James P. Introduction. *Album of the World's Gems: Photographs of the Majestic and Imposing in Nature; the Beautiful and Inspiring in Art; the Grandly Scenic, Eventfully Historic and Strikingly Descriptive; Including Impressive Scenes, Heroic Events and Famous Achievements Which Mark Human Progress and Distinguish Nations of the Earth, to Which is Added Portraits of the World's Most Famous People*. Philadelphia: Historical Publishing Company, 1893.

Brunialti, Carla Ginelli and Roberto. *A Tribute to America: Costume Jewelry 1935-1950*. Milan: EDITA, 2002.

Bruton, LaRee Johnson. *Ladies Vintage Accessories Identification & Value Guide*. Paducah Kentucky: Collector Books, 2001.

Burack, Benjamin. *Ivory and Its Uses*. New York: Charles E. Tuttle Company, 1984.

Burkholz, Matthew L., and Linda Lichenberg Kaplan. *Copper Art Jewelry, a Different Lustre*. West Chester, Pennsylvania: Schiffer Publishing Ltd., 1992.

Burgess, Fred W. *Antique Jewelry and Trinkets*. New York: Tudor Publishing Company, 1919.

Bushman, Richard L. *The Refinement of America; Persons, Houses, Cities*. New York: Vintage Books, 1993.

Brands, H. W. *The Age of Gold: The California Gold Rush and the New American Dream*. New York: Doubleday, 2002.

Bradford, Ernle. *English Victorian Jewelry*. Middlesex: Spring Books, 1967 (first published 1959 by Country Life Ltd).

Brunor, Martin. *The Practical Electroplater: A Comprehensive Treatise on Electroplating, with Notes on Ancient and Modern Gilding, and Formulas for New Solutions*. New York: Emile Brunor, Publisher, 1894.

Callan, Georgina O'Hara. New York: Thames & Hudson, Inc., 1998.

Carroll, Julia C. *Collecting Costume Jewelry 101*. Paducah, Kentucky: Collector Books, 2004.

Carpenter, Charles H., Jr. with Mary Grace Carpenter. *Tiffany Silver*. New York: Dodd, Mead & Company, 1978.

Cera, Deanna Farneti. *Amazing Gems: An Illustrated Guide to the World's Most Dazzling Costume Jewelry*. New York: Harry N. Abrams, Inc., Publishers, 1995.

Chamberlain, Basil Hall, and W. B. Mason. *A Handbook for Travellers in Japan*. London: John Murray, 1894.

Chase, A. W. Dr. *Chase's Recipes; or Information for Everybody: An Invaluable Collection of About Eight Hundred Practical Recipes for Merchants, Grocers, Saloon-Keepers, Physicians, Druggists, Tanners, Shoe Makers, Harness Makers, Painters, Jewelers, Blacksmiths, Tinners, Gunsmiths, Farriers, Barbers, Bakers, Dyers, Renovators, Farmers, and Families Generally*. 35th ed. Ann Arbor, Michigan: A. W. Chase, M. D. Publisher, 1866.

Cheem, Aliph. *Lays of Ind*. 7th ed. London: Thacker, Spink and Co., 1883.

Clark, Tessa, ed. *Bakelite Style*. London: Quintet Publishing Limited, 1997.

Corbett, Patricia. *Verdura: the Life and Work of a Master Jeweler*. New York: Harry N. Abrams, Inc., 2002.

Copeland, Lawrence L., ed. *Diamonds...Famous, Notable and Unique*. United States: Gemological Institute of America, 1966.

Corgnati, Martina. *Mario Buccellati: Prince of Goldsmiths*. New York: Rizzoli International Publications, Inc., 1999.

Crosby, Deborah. *Victorian Pencils: Tools to Jewels*. Atglen, Pennsylvania: Schiffer Publishing, Ltd., 1998.

Crosby, Deborah. *Silver Novelties in the Gilded Age*. Atglen, Pennsylvania: Schiffer Publishing, Ltd., 2001.

Cummins, Genevieve E., and Nerylla D. Taunton. *Chatelaines: Utility to Extravagance.* Woodbridge, Suffolk: Antique Collectors' Club, 1996.

Darbyshire, Lydia, ed. *Jewelry: A Visual Celebration of the World's Great Jewelry-Making Traditions.* Edison, New Jersey: Chartwell Books, 1996.

DeLorme, Maureen. *Mourning Art & Jewelry.* Atglen, Pennsylvania: Schiffer Publishing Ltd., 2004.

Dickinson, Joan Y. *The Book of Diamonds.* New York: Dover Publications, 2001. Originally published by Crown Publishers, 1965.

Dietz, Ulysses Grant, Jenna Weissman Joselit, Kevin J. Smead, and Janet Zapata. *The Glitter & The Gold: Fashioning America's Jewelry.* Newark, New Jersey: The Newark Museum, 1997.

Dolan, Maryanne. *Collecting Rhinestone Colored Jewelry.* Florence, Alabama: Books Americana, 1989.

Dolan, Maryanne. *Vintage Clothing, 1880-1960.* 2nd ed. Florence, Alabama: Books Americana, 1987.

Dunlop, M. H. *Scandal and Sensation in Turn-of-the-Century New York.* New York: Perennial, Harper Collins Publishers, 2001.

Duprène, Maurice. *305 Authentic Art Nouveau Jewelry Designs.* New York: Dover Publications, Inc., 1985.

Drucker, Janet. *Georg Jensen: A Tradition of Splendid Silver.* 2nd ed. Atglen, Pennsylvania: Schiffer Publishing, Ltd., 2001.

Edmunds, Will H. *Pointers and Clues to the Subjects of Chinese and Japanese Art.* Chicago: Art Media Resources, Ltd. (republished from a 1934 edition).

Egger, Gerhart. *Generations of Jewelry, From the 15th Through the 20th Century.* West Chester, Pennsylvania: Schiffer Publishing Ltd., 1988.

Ely, Richard T. *Evolution of Industrial Society.* New York: The Chautauqua Press, 1903.

Emmet, Boris, and John E. Jeuck. *Catalogs and Counters: A History of Sears, Roebuck & Company.* Chicago: The University of Chicago Press, 1950.

Ettinger, Roseann. *Forties and Fifties Popular Jewelry.* Atglen, Pennsylvania: Schiffer Publishing Ltd., 1994.

Ettinger, Roseann. *Popular Jewelry 1840-1940.* 2nd ed. Atglen, Pennsylvania: Schiffer Publishing, Ltd., 1997.

Everitt, Sally and David Lancaster. *Christie's Twentieth-Century Jewelry.* New York: Watson-Guptill Publications, 2002.

Fales, Martha Gandy. *Jewelry in America.* Woodbridge, Suffolk: Antique Collectors' Club, 1995.

Fischer, Lucy. *Designing Women: Cinema, Art Deco, & the Female Form.* New York: Columbia University Press, 2003.

Flint, Charles L.; McCay, C. F.; Merriam, J. C; et al. *One Hundred Years' Progress of the United States...with Marvels That Our Grandchildren Will See...* Hartford: L. Stebbins, 1880.

Flower, Margaret. *Victorian Jewelry.* Mineola, New York: Dover Publications, 2002. First published 1951 by Cassell & Company, London.

Foresta, Merry A. *American Photographs: The First Century.* Washington, D.C.: Smithsonian Institution Press, 1996.

Fowler, Marian. *Adventures of a Diamond: Hope.* New York: Ballantine Books, 2002.

Gay, Peter. *The Tender Passion: The Bourgeois Experience: Victoria to Freud.* New York: W. W. Norton & Company, 1986.

Giafferi, Paul Louis de. *L'Histoire du Costume Feminin Mondial La Magnificence des Habillements Egyptiens.* n.d. (circa 1920), n.p.

Gee, George E. *Gold Alloys.* London: Crosby, Lockwood and Son, 1929.

Giles, Stephen, consultant. *Miller's Antiques Checklist: Jewelry.* London: Octopus Publishing, Ltd., 1997, reissued 2000.

Gernsheim, Alison. *Victorian and Edwardian Fashion: A Photographic Survey.* New York: Dover Publications, 1981.

Gordon, Angie. *Twentieth Century Costume Jewelry.* London: ADASIA INTERNATIONAL, 1990.

Gordon, Cathy, and Sheila Pamfiloff. *Miriam Haskell Jewelry.* Atglen, Pennsylvania: Schiffer Publishing Ltd., 2004.

Gordon, H. Panmure. *The Land of the Almighty Dollar.* London: Frederick Warne & Co., 1892.

Greenbaum, Toni. *Messengers of Modernism: American Studio Jewelry 1940-1960.* New York: Flammarion, 1996.

Greenhalgh, Paul, ed. *Art Nouveau 1890-1914.* London: V. & A. Publications, 2000.

Guaralnick, Peter. *The Rise of Elvis Presley: Last Train to Memphis.* New York: Little, Brown and Company, 1994.

Hackney, Ki and Diana Edkins. *People & Pearls: The Magic Endures.* New York: HarperCollins Publishers, Inc., 2000.

Halttunen, Karen. *Confidence Men and Painted Ladies: A Study of Middle-Class Culture in America, 1830-1870.* New Haven: Yale University Press, 1982.

Heady, Sue. *Jewels.* London: PRC Publishing Ltd., 1999.

Heady, Sue. *Emeralds Are a Girl's Best Friend.* Edison, New Jersey: Chartwell Books, Inc., 1999.

Henzel, S. Sylvia. *Collectible Costume Jewelry ID and Value Guide.* Iola, Wisconsin: Krause Publications, 1997.

History of the Jewelers' Security Alliance of the United States, 1883-1958. The Jewelers' Security Alliance of the United States, 1958.

Hosley, William. *The Japan Idea: Art and Life in Victorian America.* Hartford, Connecticut: Wadsworth Athenaeum, 1990.

Hothem, Lar. *North American Indian Artifacts,* 6th edition. Iola, Wisconsin: Krause Publications, 1998.

Husfloen, Kyle, ed. *Antique Trader Jewelry Price Guide.* Iola, Wisconsin: Krause Publications, 2001.

Ingram, J. S. *The Centennial Exposition, Described and Illustrated, Being a Concise and Graphic Description of this Grand Enterprise, Commemorative of the First Centenary of the American Independence.* Philadelphia: Hubbard Bros., 1876.

James, Duncan. *Antique Jewelry: Its Manufacture, Materials, and Design.* Buckinghamshire: Shire Publications Ltd., 2nd edition, 1998.

Jargstorf, Sibylle. *Baubles, Buttons and Beads: The Heritage of Bohemia.* Atglen, Pennsylvania: Schiffer Publishing Ltd., 1993.

Johnson, Anna. *Handbags: The Power of the Purse.* New York: Workman Publishing, 2002.

Jones, Julie and Heidi King. *Gold of the Americas.* New York: The Metropolitan Museum of Art, 2002.

Karlin, Elyse Zorn. *Jewelry & Metalwork in the Arts & Crafts Tradition.* Atglen, Pennsylvania: Schiffer Publishing Ltd., 1993 & 2004.

Katz, Sylvia. *Early Plastics.* Buckinghamshire: Shire Publications Ltd., 2nd edition, 1994.

King, Moses. *Notable New Yorkers 1896-1899.* New York: Bartlett & Company, the Orr Press, 1899.

Koch, Michael and Evelyne Possémé, Judy Rodoe, Geoffrey Munn, Maire-Noël de Gary, Barbara Furrer, Catherine Arminjon, Alexander Herog von Württemberg. *The Belle Epoque of French Jewelry 1850-1910.* London: Thomas Heneage & Co Limited, 1989.

Kunz, George Frederick. *The Curious Lore of Precious Stones.* New York: Halcyon House, 1938.

Lambert, Sylvie. *The Ring.* Switzerland: RotoVision SA, 1998.

Landman, Neil H., Paula M. Mikkelsen, Rudiger Biehler, and Bennet Bronson. *Pearls: A Natural History.* New York: Harry N. Abrams, Inc., 2001.

Laurie, Bruce. *Artisans Into Workers.* Chicago: University of Illinois Press, 1997.

Lehnert, Gertrud. *Fashion: An Historical Overview.* Barron's Educational Series, Inc., 1998.

Leshner, Leigh. *Vintage Jewelry: A Price Identification Guide 1020-1940s.* Iola, Wisconsin: Krause Publications, 2002.

Lisle, Laurie. *Louise Nevelson: A Passionate Life.* Lincoln, NE: iUniverse.com, Inc., 2000 (originally published by Summit Books in 1990).

Loar, Peggy, foreword by. *Art Nouveau Bing; Paris Style 1900.* New York: Harry N. Abrams, Inc., Publishers, 1986.

Loring, John. *Tiffany's 20th Century: A Portrait of American Style.* New York: Harry N. Abrams, Publishers, 1997.

Loring, John. *Tiffany Jewels.* New York: Harry N. Abrams, Publishers, 1999.

Loring, John. *Louis Comfort Tiffany at Tiffany & Co.* New York: Harry N. Abrams, Incorporated, 2002.

Loring, John. *Tiffany in Fashion.* New York: Harry N. Abrams, 2003.

Loring, John. *Tiffany Fauna and Tiffany Flora.* New York: Harry N. Abrams, Inc., Publishers, 2003.

Lynnlee, J. L. *All That Glitters.* Revised edition. Atglen, Pennsylvania: Schiffer Publishing, Ltd., 1986.

Mace, O. Henry. *Collector's Guide to Early Photographs.* 2nd edition. Iola, Wisconsin: Krause Publications, 1999.

Mackey, Albert. *The History of Freemasonry: Its Legendary Origins.* New York: Portland House, an imprint of Random House Value Publishing, Inc., 2002.

Madsen, Axel. *Chanel: A Woman of Her Own.* New York: Henry Holt and Company, 1990.

Malaguzzi, Silvia. *The Pearl.* New York: Rizzoli International Publications, Inc., 2000.

Marzio, Peter C. *The Democratic Art: An Exhibition of the History of Chromolithography in America 1840-1900.* Fort Worth, Texas: Amon Carter Museum of Western Art, 1979.

Mascetti, Daniela, and Amanda Triossi. *Bulgari.* New York: Abbeville Press Publishers, 1996.

Marshall, Suzanne. *200 Years of American Manufactured Jewelry & Accessories.* Atglen, Pennsylvania: Schiffer Publishing Ltd., 2003.

Mauriés, Patrick. *Jewelry by Chanel.* New York: Little, Brown and Company, 2000.

Mayer, Barbara. *In the Arts & Crafts Style.* San Francisco: Chronicle Books, 1992.

McConnell, Sophie. *Metropolitan Jewelry.* New York: Metropolitan Museum of Art and Bullfinch Press, 1991.

Meilach, Dona Z. *Ethnic Jewelry: Design & Inspiration for Collectors & Craftsmen.* New York: Crown Publishers, Inc., 1981.

Miller, Anna M. *The Buyer's Guide to Affordable Antique Jewelry.* New York: Carol Publishing Group, 1993.

Miller, Anna M. *Cameos, Old and New* (3rd edition). Woodstock, Vermont: GemStone Press, 2002.

Miller, Horace. *Faking It.*

Miller, Judith. *Collector's Guide: Costume Jewelry.* New York: DK Publishing, 2003.

Millidge, Judith, ed. *Art Deco Fashion and Jewelry.* Kent, England: Grange Books, 1998.

Millidge, Judith. *Art Nouveau Jewellery and Metalwork.* Kent, England: Grange Books, 1998.

Miller, Harrice Simons. *Official Price Guide to Costume Jewelry.* 3rd ed. New York: House of Collectibles, The Crown Publishing Group, 2002.

Moore, R. *The Universal Assistant and Complete Mechanic.* Bridgeport, Connecticut: Frederick Keppy, Scientific Book Publisher,1881.

Moro, Ginger. *European Designer Jewelry.* Atglen, Pennsylvania: Schiffer Publishing Ltd., 1995.

Morrill, Penny C., curator. *William Spratling and the Mexican Silver Renaissance.* New York: Harry N. Abrams, Inc., 2002.

Mossman, Susan, editor. *Early Plastics: Perspectives 1850-1950.* Washington: Leicester University Press, 1997.

Mulvagh, Jane. *Costume Jewelry in Vogue.* New York: Thames and Hudson Inc., 1988.

Newman, Harold. *An Illustrated Dictionary of Jewelry.* London: Thames and Hudson, Ltd., 1981.

Newman, Harold. *An Illustrated Dictionary of Silverware.* London: Thames and Hudson, Ltd., 1987.

Nichols, Sarah. *Aluminum by Design.* Pittsburgh: Carnegie Museum of Art, 2000.

Nissenson, Marilyn, and Susan Jonas. *Snake Charm.* New York: Harry N. Abrams, Inc., Publishers, 1995.

Nissenson, Marilyn, and Susan Jonas. *Jeweled Bugs and Butterflies.* New York: Harry N. Abrams, Inc., Publishers, 2000.

Patch, Susanne Steinem. *Blue Mystery: The Story of the Hope Diamond.* New York: Harry N. Abrams, Inc., 1999.

Papi, Stefano and Alexandra Rhodes. *Famous Jewelry Collectors.* New York: Harry N. Abrams, Inc., 1999.

Phillips, Clare. *Jewelry From Antiquity to the Present.* London: Thames and Hudson, Ltd., 1996.

Pitman, Ann Mitchell. *Inside the Jewelry Box, A Collector's Guide to Costume Jewelry.* Paducah, Kentucky: Collector Books, 2004.

Price, Judith. *Masterpieces of American Jewelry.* Philadelphia: Running Press, 2004.

Purtell, Joseph. *The Tiffany Touch.* New York: Random House, Inc., 1971.

Ragot, Vincent-Emmanuel. *Gianmaria Buccellati.* New York: Assouline Publishing, n.d.

Rainwater, Dorothy T. and Judy Redfield. *Encyclopedia of American Silver Manufacturers.* Revised fourth edition. Atglen, Pennsylvania: Schiffer Publishing Ltd., 1998.

Raulet, Sylvie. *Art Deco Jewelry.* Thames and Hudson Inc., first paperback edition, 2002. Originally published in French, 1984.

Rezazadeh, Fred. *Costume Jewelry, a Practical Handbook & Value Guide.* Paducah, Kentucky: Collector Books, 1998 (values updated 2000).

Rezazadeh, Fred. *Collectible Silver Jewelry Identification and Value Guide.* Paducah, Kentucky: Collector Books, 2001.

Ripley, George and Charles A. Dana. *The American Cyclopedia.* Revised edition. New York: D. Appleton and Company, 1874.

Romaine, Lawrence B. *A Guide to American Trade Catalogs.* Minneola, New York: Dover Publications, Inc., 1990.

Romero, Christine. *Warman's Jewelry.* 2nd ed. Iola, Wisconsin: Krause Publications, 1998.

Romero, Christine. *Warman's Jewelry.* 3rd ed. Iola, Wisconsin: Krause Publications, 2003.

Rudoe, Judy. *Cartier's 1900-1939.* New York: Harry N. Abrams, Inc., Publishers, 1997.

Sacks, Oliver. *Uncle Tungsten: Memories of a Chemical Boyhood.* New York: First Vintage Books Edition, 2002.

Salmon, Béatrice (preface). *Luxe et Fantaisie: Bijoux de la collection Barbara Berger.* Paris: Musèe de la Mode, 2003.

Salsbery, David and Lee. *ABCs of Costume Jewelry.* Atglen, Pennsylvania: Schiffer Publishing Ltd, 2003.

Schiffer, Nancy. *The Power of Jewelry.* West Chester, Pennsylvania: Schiffer Publishing Ltd., 1988.

Schiffer, Nancy N. *Silver Jewelry Treasures.* Atglen, Pennsylvania: Schiffer Publishing, Ltd., 1993.

Schiffer, Nancy N. *Rhinestones!* Atglen, Pennsylvania: Schiffer Publishing, Ltd., 1993.

Schiffer, Nancy N. *Silver Jewelry Designs: Evaluating Quality, Good, Better, Best.* Atglen, Pennsylvania: Schiffer Publishing, Ltd., 1993.

Schiffer, Nancy N. *Costume Jewelry: the Fun of Collecting,* revised edition. Atglen, Pennsylvania: Schiffer Publishing, Ltd., 2001.

Schlereth, Thomas J. *Victorian America: Transformations in Everyday Life.* New York: Harper Perennial, 1991.

Schon, Marbeth. *Modernist Jewelry 1930-1960.* Atglen, Pennsylvania: Schiffer Publishing Ltd., 2004

Schumann, Walter. *Gemstones of the World.* Revised and expanded edition. New York: Sterling Publishing Co., Inc., n.d.

Schwartz, Joanne. *Charms and Charm Bracelets.* Atglen, Pennsylvania: Schiffer Publishing Ltd., 2005.

Shugart, Cooksey, Tom Engle, Richard E. Gilbert. *Complete Price Guide to Watches, 2001.* Cleveland, Tennessee: Cooksey Shugart Publications, 2001.

Silliman, Benjamin. *Elements Of Chemistry.* 2 vol. New Haven, Connecticut: Hezekiah Howe, 1831.

Simonds, Cherri. *Collectible Costume Jewelry.* Paducah, Kentucky: Collector Books, 1997.

Slack, Charles. *Noble Obsession: Charles Goodyear, Thomas Hancock, and the Race to Unlock the Greatest Industrial Secret of the Nineteenth Century.* New York: Hyperion, 2002.

Slaughter, John Robert (introduction). *Our American Century: Decade of*

Triumph: The '40s. Alexandria, Virginia: Time-Life Books, 1999.

Sleffel, Charles Conrad. *Working in Metals.* New York: Doubleday, Page & Company, 1911.

Snider, Nick. *Sweetheart Jewelry and Collectibles.* Atglen, Pennsylvania: Schiffer Publishing Ltd., 1995.

Spencer, Dorothy. *Found Object Art.* Atglen, Pennsylvania: Schiffer Publishing Ltd., 2002.

Steele, Valerie. *The Fan.* New York: Rizzoli International Publications, Inc., 2002.

Taylor, Elizabeth. *My Love Affair With Jewelry.* New York: Simon & Schuster, 2002.

Tennenbaum, Suzanne, and Janet Zapata. *The Jeweled Menagerie: The World of Animals in Gems.* New York: Thames & Hudson, 2001.

Trademarks of the Jewelry and Kindred Trades. New York: The Jewelers' Circular Publishing Co., 1898.

Trademarks of the Jewelry and Kindred Trades. New York: The Jewelers' Circular Publishing Co., 1922.

Tretiack, Phillippe. *Cartier.* New York: UNIVERSE PUBLISHING, 1997.

Twitchell, James B. *Living it Up: Our Love Affair with Luxury.* New York: Columbia University Press, 2001.

Vaill, Amanda and Janet Zapata. *Seaman Schepps: A Century of New York Jewelry Design.* New York: The Vendome Press, 2004.

Van Cleve, B. Frank. *The English and American Mechanic.* Philadelphia: B. Frank Van Cleve Publisher, 1874.

Von Habsburg, Géza. *Princely Treasures.* New York: The Vendome Press, 1997.

Ward, Barbara McLean and Gerald W. R. Wood, editors. *Silver in American Life.* Boston: David R. Godine Publisher in Association with the Yale University Art Gallery and the American Federation for the Arts, 1979.

Wasserstrom, Donna, and Leslie Piña. *Bakelite Jewelry: Good, Better, Best.* Atglen, Pennsylvania: Schiffer Publishing Ltd., 1997.

Wehde, Albert. *Chasing and Repoussé.* Chicago: The Tremonia Publishing Company, 1924.

Whiteway, Michael, ed. *Shock of the Old: Christopher Dresser's Design Revolution.* London: V & A Publications in association with Cooper-Hewitt, National Design Museum, 2004.

Whitlock, Herbert P. *The Story of the Gems.* New York: Garden City Publishing Co., Inc., 1940.

Woshner, Mike. *India Rubber and Gutta Percha in the Civil War Era.* Alexandria, Virginia: O'Donnell Publications, 1999.

Wright, Richardson. *Hawkers & Walkers in Early America.* Philadelphia: J. B. Lippincott, 1927.

Young, Louisa. *The Book of the Heart.* New York: Doubleday, 2003.

Zabar, Tracey. *Charmed Bracelets.* New York: Stewart, Tabori & Chang, 2004.

Catalogues

The A. C. Becken 12th Annual Illustrated Catalogue and Price List. Chicago: Becken, 1903.

The 1934 Becken Book: Continuing Otto Young & Co. and C. H. Knights-Thearle Co. Chicago: Jas. W. Clark, 1933.

Catalog No. 11 Wm. Kendrick's Sons Jewelers and Silversmiths. Louisville, Kentucky, 1908.

Crosby M'F'G Co., n.d. circa 1900.

Illustrated Catalog. J. Lynn & Co., New York, n. d.

R. Pearlman, Inc., Modern Creations in Gold and Platinum. New York: Florentine Press, n. d.

Wm. J. Fraser, Illustrated Catalogue, 1892. Lincoln, Pennsylvania: no publisher listed, 1892.

Yearbook for 1910. Daniel Low and Company, Salem, Massachusetts, 1910.

Websites

Aluminum
http://www.world-aluminium.org/
http://www.carnegiemuseums.org/cmag/bk_issue/1997/sepoct/dept7.html
http://www.aluminumbydesign.org/pages/tours_html/jewelry_to_jets/1.htm

Glossary
http://www.allaboutjewels.com/

Political Buttons
http://www.msys.net/cress/refernc/glossary/htm
http://www.philadelphiahistory.org/pages/vote.html

Pinback Buttons
http://www.antiquetintoy.com/notesbyt.htm

Ma Winkle
http://www.old-time.com/premiums/radiopremiums 12.html

Dennis Morgan
http://www.loc.gov/film/taves8.html

National Association of Letter Carriers
http://www.nalc.org/

United Office and Professional Workers of America
http://www.opeiu.org/

Robbins Company, Attleboro Massachusetts
http://www.nben.org/HTMLSrc/Resources/OTAcases/robbins.html
http://www.therobbinsco.com/NewsFinalMerger.html

Periodicals

The Century Illustrated Monthly Magazine, vol. LIX, no. 2, December, 1899.

The Cosmopolitan, vol. XXXVI, no. 1, November, 1903.

The Cosmopolitan, vol. XXXVI, no. 2, December 1903.

Demorest's Monthly Magazine, Vol. 13, January-December 1879.

Harper's Bazar, Vol. XIV, no. 1, January 1, 1881.

Harper's New Monthly Magazine, no. CLXXVIII, March, 1865

Harper's New Monthly Magazine, no. 188, January, 1866.

McClure's Magazine, November, 1908.

Index

A younger generation of vintage jewelry enthusiasts!